Dedication

To all the leaders who have ever hidden in the bathroom for a moment of peace, to the ones who've nodded knowingly in meetings while internally screaming, and to the brave souls who've confidently said, "Leave it with me," and then Googled what they were actually supposed to do.

This book is for you—the unsung heroes who've mastered the art of looking slightly more knowledgeable than a Wikipedia article and who understand that sometimes the best leadership strategy is a well-timed coffee break.

And to my own team, who have patiently endured my 'inspirational' speeches and still miraculously manage to show up every day. Your ability to pretend I know what I'm doing is truly the wind beneath my wings.

Here's to embracing our imperfections and leading with a sense of humor. May our coffee be strong, our decisions be adequate, and our panic be controlled.

Foreword

To the Titans and the Titans-in-Training,

In the hallowed halls of leadership, where industry giants roam and workaholics flourish like weeds in an over-ambitious garden, I've had the dubious honor of rubbing shoulders with the crème de la crème. Schooled among the elite, where excellence is the appetizer and perfection the main course, I've witnessed a parade of impeccable leaders – each more flawless than the last... or so it seemed.

But here's the twist: under the microscope of my ever-curious, sometimes skeptical eye, these paragons of leadership revealed something wonderfully human. They were, in fact, perfectly imperfect. And so, amid the glittering successes and sky-high expectations, I discovered the truth – the meticulously maintained façade of perfection is about as real as the Tooth Fairy.

You see, behind every decision that's touted as strategic genius lurks a frantic Google search; behind every inspiring speech, a moment of 'what in the world am I even saying?'; and behind every composed leader, a slightly frazzled individual wondering if they left the coffee pot on.

This book is born from a lifetime of observing the high and mighty lose their capes in the wind – and learning that, frankly, it's okay. My journey has woven through the pinnacle of industry, where I've shared coffee (and occasional existential crises) with those deemed the best of the best. Yet, in the silence of their offices, I've seen the weight of perfection bend even the sturdiest of backs.

But let's not forget the unsung heroes – the everyday warriors clocking in to earn their daily bread. Those who dream not of conquering empires but of a decent day's work followed by the sweet escape of a Netflix binge. It's for them, and perhaps for you, that I pen these words.

In the sanctified halls of top-tier schools, where I was groomed alongside the future leaders of tomorrow (who, by the way, are just as baffled by adulting as the rest of us), I realized something revolutionary. Normalcy is underrated. 'Good enough' isn't a compromise; it's the secret ingredient for a sustainable, healthy life both at work and beyond.

So, as you turn these pages, prepare to dismantle the myth of perfection. Embrace the chaos, chuckle at the confusion, and join me in a toast to the perfectly imperfect art of leadership. Because, my friends, in the grand scheme of things, we're all just trying to work to live, not live to work.

Here's to finding joy in the 'good enough,' and remember – if all else fails, there's always chocolate.

Yours in Adequate Leadership,

Thomas P Huber, PhD, MS ECS

Introduction: Congratulations, You're Flawed!

Welcome, my fellow flawed beings, to the grand gala of imperfection in leadership – a place where stumbling is the new running and where every misstep is a cha-cha in disguise.

Let me begin by congratulating you, dear reader, on your impeccable choice of this book. It's not every day that one stumbles upon a treasure trove that celebrates the art of being gloriously average in leadership. Here, we don't just embrace flaws; we give them a standing ovation.

Picture this: A leader, let's call him Mr. Perfect. He walks into a room, and the air practically shimmers with his flawlessness. His hair – a masterpiece. His suit – a sartorial triumph. His smile – could sell ice to penguins. He begins his speech, and it's like listening to the sweet serenade of a well-tuned leadership symphony. But then, disaster strikes. Mr. Perfect, in his stride of confidence, trips over the most formidable adversary known to mankind – his own shoelaces.

As Mr. Perfect tumbles, his aura of perfection shatters into a million little imperfect pieces. And in that moment, he becomes one of us – a beautifully flawed leader, trying to navigate the tightrope of management without falling headfirst into the cake of chaos.

This book, dear reader, is your invitation to the world where such tumbles are not just expected but celebrated. It's an ode to all the Mr. and Ms. Perfects out there who have realized that trying to maintain an image of infallibility is about as easy as teaching a cat to swim.

So, as you turn these pages, prepare to laugh, nod in agreement, and maybe even wince a bit as we explore the wonderfully wonky realm of imperfect leadership. We'll delve into the joys of mediocrity, the beauty of the blunder, and the sheer exhilaration of not having all the answers.

Remember, in the world of leadership, perfection is a myth, and your flaws are the badges of your humanity. Wear them proudly. After all, in the circus of leadership, it's the clowns who often have the most fun. Welcome to the celebration of imperfection. May your leadership journey be adequately average, and your missteps be as graceful as a three-legged dance.

The Myth of the Flawless Leader

Ah, the Flawless Leader – a mythical creature, more elusive than a unicorn playing hide-and-seek in a field of four-leaf clovers. In the fantastical world of traditional leadership books and seminars, this paragon of virtue and skill strides among us mere mortals, a beacon of infallibility. But let's be honest: believing in the Flawless Leader is akin to waiting for a leprechaun to lead you to a pot of gold at the end of a rainbow.

These books and seminars would have you believe that the perfect leader wakes up every morning with a halo of strategic insight, dons armor forged in the fires of unwavering confidence, and sallies forth to conquer the corporate world with a single, impeccably manicured hand. The other hand, presumably, is busy penning motivational quotes for LinkedIn.

Let's face it – most leadership advice out there is about as realistic as finding a diet that lets you lose weight by eating nothing but chocolate eclairs. They peddle a vision of leadership where you can, and should, juggle seventeen tasks while balancing on a unicycle, all the time exuding an aura of calm control that would put Zen monks to shame.

These gurus of leadership perfection talk about never making a mistake, always having the right answer, and leading teams with the effortlessness of a maestro conducting a symphony in his sleep. If you've ever actually led a team, you know this is about as achievable as teaching a cat to fetch your morning newspaper.

The truth is, most leaders are winging it to some degree. We're all in a perpetual state of 'fake it till we make it,' interspersed with moments of 'I have absolutely no idea what I'm doing, but let's see how this goes.' Leadership isn't a serene sail across a calm sea; it's more like building a boat while you're already out in the water, during a storm, and your crew is asking you where the life jackets are.

Let us take a moment to laugh in the face of these impossibly high standards. Embrace your inner flawed leader, for it is your imperfections that make you relatable, approachable, and, dare I say, a more effective leader. After all, when was the last time you related to someone who claimed they'd never once messed up?

In the following pages, we'll continue to debunk these myths, one laugh at a time. Buckle up; it's going to be a hilariously bumpy ride!

What This Book is (and isn't)

Welcome, dear reader, to a section I like to call "Setting the Record Crooked." Before we embark on this rollercoaster of leadership follies, let's get one thing straight – or rather, comfortably skewed. This book isn't a magic potion to transform you into a superhuman leader with the strength of Hercules and the wisdom of Athena. If that's what you're after, I believe you've wandered into the wrong literary aisle.

Now, if you're looking for a tome that will make you a more tolerable human being to be around – bingo! You've hit the jackpot. This book is less about crafting the perfect leader and more about embracing the perfectly adequate one. The one who knows their coffee order better than their five-year strategic plan.

In my early career, I was the maestro of micromanaging. I could orchestrate an office with the precision of a Swiss watch – and the flexibility of one, too. Telling people what to do wasn't just a job; it was an art form. But, as time went by, I evolved from micromanager extraordinaire to a leader who occasionally wonders if 'delegate' is just a fancy word for 'defer until forgotten.' If there's one thing I've learned, it's that the journey from overbearing overseer to laissez-faire legend is filled with a generous dose of reality checks (and a few lost emails).

As you turn these pages, expect a healthy dose of self-deprecating humor, a pinch of sarcasm, and a sprinkle of not-so-serious advice. This book is your guide to becoming a leader who's not necessarily revered, but at least not actively avoided at office gatherings.

We won't promise you the moon, but we might be able to locate a decent flashlight to help you find your way in the dark corridors of leadership. Expect to find anecdotes that make you chuckle, advice that makes you ponder, and perhaps the odd epiphany that makes you say, "Huh, I guess I could try that."

This book is a celebration of the average, a tribute to the 'good enough,' and a high-five to all the leaders out there making it up as they go along. Let's toss out the leadership rulebook and write our own – one that's a little less rigid and a lot more fun.

Why 'Good Enough' is Great

Ah, 'good enough' – the two words that have been the silent champions of leaders everywhere. It's time to pull back the curtain on this unsung hero of leadership philosophy. 'Good enough' isn't just about setting the bar at a reachable height; it's about acknowledging that sometimes the bar doesn't even need to be there.

Let me confess – there was a time when I aimed for the stars, only to realize I was afraid of heights. I aspired to be the Michelangelo of the boardroom, crafting corporate masterpieces. But let's face it, sometimes you don't need the Sistine Chapel; a well-painted garage will do just fine.

I remember a project early in my career that I tackled with the zeal of a knight on a quest. I was determined to make it ground-breaking, earth-shattering, universe-aligning! The result? A very impressive, thoroughly detailed, and utterly unnecessary 50-page report that could have been summed up in a two-paragraph email. That was when it hit me – perfection is overrated, and 'good enough' can be absolutely liberating.

Let's consider the 'good enough' leader. This magnificent creature navigates the corporate jungle with the grace of a slightly disoriented gazelle. They understand that sometimes, a decision made is better than a decision marinated. They're the ones who say, "Let's just go with it and see what happens," and then actually manage to sleep at night.

Now, aiming for 'good enough' isn't about being mediocre or lazy. It's about being realistic. It's about understanding that the perfect plan doesn't exist outside of those overpriced leadership books. It's about knowing that sometimes the best course of action is to take a deep breath, pick a direction, and stride confidently into the unknown – or at least into the next meeting.

'Good enough' leadership is the art of balancing ambition with sanity. It's recognizing that you might not change the world by Thursday, but you can certainly improve a small corner of your office. It's about celebrating the small victories, like when a meeting ends on time, or when the coffee machine actually works.

So, let's raise a glass (or a lukewarm mug of office coffee) to 'good enough.' To the leaders who are brave enough to say, "This is fine," and mean it. May your inbox be manageable, your decisions be adequate, and your peace of mind be plentiful.

A Tour of the Chapters

Buckle up, dear reader, for a whirlwind tour of our chapters – a journey through the hilariously haphazard world of leadership, where the insights are real, but the promises are dubious. Each chapter is a blend of wit, wisdom, and a dash of whimsy, designed to make you think, chuckle, and maybe even cringe a little.

- Chapter 1 – "Congratulations, You're Flawed!"
  Dive headfirst into the wonderful world of imperfect leadership. It's like a welcome party where everyone's awkward, and the punchline is that nobody's perfect.

- Chapter 2 - "Mistakes: The Unexpected Secret Weapon"
  Discover the art of turning blunders into wonders. Remember, every mistake is just a misfired attempt at greatness (or at least a good story for later).

- Chapter 3 - "The 'Good Enough' Leader's Survival Kit"
  Unpack a survival kit filled with gadgets for the 'adequately average' leader. Think of it as a Swiss Army knife, but instead of tools, it's full of excuses and diversions.

- Chapter 4 - "Delegation: Because Laziness Can Be Efficient"
  Learn how to delegate like a pro – or at least like someone who's really good at pretending to be busy. It's about empowering others (and enjoying your coffee in peace).

- Chapter 5 – "Feedback: How to Smile While Being Criticized"
  Master the art of receiving feedback with a smile, even when it feels like a pat on the back with a cactus. It's all about grinning and bearing it.

- Chapter 6 - "The Fine Art of Mediocre Decision Making"
  Discover why sometimes the best decision is a half-baked one. After all, who needs a fully cooked idea when a doughy one will suffice?

- Chapter 7 - "Perfection: The Fast Track to a Nervous Breakdown"

Explore the hilariously high stakes of chasing perfection. Spoiler alert: it's a bit like chasing your tail, but less productive.

- Chapter 8 - "Embracing the Chaos: A Leader's Guide to Controlled Panic"
  Embrace the chaos of leadership with a guide to managing panic with poise. It's like juggling flaming swords, except the swords are emails, and the flames are your to-do list.

- Chapter 9 - "The Leader's Guide to Faking It Until You Make It"
  Learn the fine art of faking confidence till you actually feel it. It's for those who believe that if you can't make it, just fake it – with flair.

- Chapter 10 - "The Joy of Lowered Expectations"
  Revel in the joy of setting the bar low and still managing to trip over it. It's about finding the fun in being fundamentally flawed.

On this expedition of eccentric expertise, remember, behind every chuckle is a nugget of truth, and behind every sarcasm-laced comment, a genuine insight. Let's laugh our way through leadership, one page at a time.

Setting the Expectations Low (But Not Too Low)

As we stand on the precipice of embarking on our unorthodox journey through the world of leadership, let me set the expectations – low, but not subterranean. Consider this book the limbo bar at the leadership party; we're aiming to get under it without throwing our backs out.

Leadership, much like a game of pin-the-tail-on-the-donkey, is often a blindfolded whirl of guesses, spins, and hopeful stabs in the right direction. This book mirrors that delightful unpredictability. It's an adventure through the leadership jungle, where the paths are winding, the maps are dubious, and the guides are... well, let's just say we're more enthusiastic than qualified.

Expect this book to be your companion in the trenches of management – the kind that hands you a shovel when you ask for a ladder. It's filled with advice that straddles the line between 'unexpectedly insightful' and 'are you sure this isn't just common sense wrapped in a joke?'

So, dear reader, prepare to embrace your imperfections, not just as tolerable quirks, but as the very essence of your leadership style. Get ready for a journey of self-discovery that's peppered with laughter, sprinkled with bewilderment, and seasoned generously with moments of "Why didn't I think of that?"

Remember, in the grand carnival of leadership, it's okay to be the merry-go-round instead of the rollercoaster. The goal here isn't to catapult you into a realm of flawless leadership. Instead, let's aim for a comfortable middle ground – where you're good enough to be effective, but still human enough to enjoy a hearty laugh at your own missteps.

Lower your expectations but keep your spirits high. With one foot in reality and the other in a comically oversized clown shoe, let's stride forth into the wonderful world of 'good enough' leadership. May your journey through these pages be as enlightening as it is entertaining!

Chapter 1: The Art of Not Knowing Everything

The Illusion of Omniscience

Picture, if you will, the 'All-Knowing Leader' – an almost mythical figure, armed with the wisdom of the ages, the foresight of a soothsayer, and the answer to every question, including the ones Google can't solve. This is the leader who, legend has it, was born with a strategic plan in one hand and a risk assessment in the other.

Let me share a tale of one such leader, Mr. Know-It-All. Mr. K, as he was fondly (or fearfully) known, never met a question he didn't have an answer to. Ask him the GDP of a remote country? He'd give you a number with two decimal places (accuracy not guaranteed). Inquire about the best marketing strategy? He'd conjure up a plan before you could finish your sentence. His team once asked him the meaning of life, half in jest. He didn't skip a beat before replying, "Efficiency."

But here's the kicker: Mr. K's unshakable confidence in his omniscience was his Achilles' heel. During a pivotal meeting, when asked about integrating a new technology, he confidently presented a plan. Little did he know, the tech had been obsolete since the days of dial-up internet. That day, the illusion shattered, and Mr. K learned a valuable lesson – not knowing everything wasn't just okay; it was normal.

You see, in their quest to embody the Oracle of Delphi, some leaders stretch the truth like it's a warm-up exercise. They'll throw in a few buzzwords, quote a couple of statistics from a study they half-read, and voila – the facade of omniscience is complete. It's like watching someone juggle flaming torches while blindfolded – impressive but bound to go up in flames sooner or later.

The irony is almost too delicious when these infallible leaders get caught in the headlights of their own unknowing. There's a certain comedic grace in watching someone who's built a tower of certainty have to use the emergency slide when it inevitably starts to wobble.

So, as we embark (not stand on the precipice) on this chapter, let's tip our hats to the beautifully flawed reality of leadership. It's a world where not knowing everything isn't a weakness; it's an invitation to learn, to collaborate, and perhaps most importantly, to have a good laugh at our own expense.

The 'I Know It All' Syndrome

Welcome to a common ailment in the leadership world: the 'I Know It All' Syndrome. This condition is as widespread in boardrooms as coffee mugs boasting "World's Best Boss." Let's diagnose the symptoms, shall we?

First up, we have the chronic inability to ask for directions. Leaders afflicted with this syndrome would rather circle the office complex for hours than admit they're lost. Their internal compass is apparently infallible – much like those of early explorers who thought they'd found India but were actually half a world away.

Then there's the acute condition of pretending to understand every acronym. In meetings, these leaders nod sagely at every mention of B2B, SEO, or ROI, even if you sneak in an LOL or a BRB. They could be drowning in a sea of abbreviations, but they'd never let on. It's like watching someone try to solve a Rubik's cube blindfolded – they're turning the blocks, but colors are definitely not aligning.

For a dash of comedic relief, let's consider a case study: Bob, a senior manager, once sat through an entire presentation about KPIs (Key Performance Indicators). He nodded, took notes, even asked insightful questions. It was leadership artistry – until he asked, "But how do these KPIs connect to the koalas per inch you mentioned earlier?" That day, Bob became a legend, a cautionary tale of the 'I Know It All' Syndrome.

The irony of the 'I Know It All' Syndrome is that it often leads to more faux pas than a sitcom character. Leaders end up like cats trying to cover up messes on a marble floor – the effort is there, but the outcome is painfully visible.

As we navigate through this chapter, remember: the first step to recovery is admitting you have a problem. And in the case of the 'I Know It All' Syndrome, it's okay to occasionally raise your hand and say, "I haven't the foggiest idea what you're talking about."

The Power of 'I Don't Know'

In the superhero league of leadership powers, 'I don't know' is the unassuming Clark Kent. It doesn't wear a cape or leap tall buildings in a single bound. Yet, it packs a punch more powerful than a locomotive – the power of humility and honesty.

Admitting ignorance is like finding a secret passage in a maze; it doesn't immediately solve the problem, but it opens up new paths. It's the anti-climax that can actually lead to a breakthrough. Picture a leader, let's call her Sarah, standing before her team, all eyes expectantly on her. The question hanging in the air is as complex as a quantum physics exam question. Sarah pauses, then with the calm confidence of someone who knows her limits, says, "I don't know, but let's find out together." The team doesn't gasp in horror; instead, they rally, ideas start flowing, and suddenly, everyone's part of the solution. It's like watching a caterpillar turn into a butterfly – a little awkward at first, but ultimately a thing of beauty.

The phrase 'I don't know' is akin to a secret handshake among the truly wise. It says, "I'm secure enough in my leadership to admit that my knowledge has gaps the size of the Grand Canyon, and that's okay." It's the anti-thesis of the 'I Know It All' Syndrome and infinitely more endearing.

Let's consider another scenario: a leader in a high-stakes meeting, faced with a question about a market trend. Instead of fabricating an answer that could potentially lead to a strategy as stable as a house of cards, they opt for the power play of 'I don't know.' Suddenly, the room shifts from expecting omniscience to appreciating honesty. It's a plot twist worthy of an Oscar.

Saying 'I don't know' may not come with a cape or a dramatic soundtrack, but it does come with its own set of superpowers. It fosters trust, encourages collaboration, and sets the stage for collective problem-solving. It's like turning on a light in a dark room – suddenly, everyone can see and contribute.

Embrace the power of 'I don't know,' and remember that it's not about glorifying ignorance, but about valuing the pursuit of knowledge. It's about swapping the illusion of infallibility for the reality of curiosity and growth. In the world of leadership, sometimes the smartest thing you can say is, "I have no idea."

Asking Questions: The Leader's Secret Weapon

If leadership were a game show, 'Asking Questions' would be the winning strategy, not 'Answering with Authority.' It's a subtle art – the Mona Lisa of management techniques. You see, the true power in leadership doesn't come from knowing all the answers; it's hidden in the craft of asking the right questions.

Think of it as the leader's Jedi mind trick. With the right question, you can steer a conversation, ignite creativity, or just buy time while you desperately try to figure out what's going on. It's like being a master puppeteer, but instead of strings, you're pulling on the threads of curiosity.

Let's break down the technique, shall we? First, there's the 'Pretend to Ponder' question. This is where you furrow your brow, tap your chin, and say something like, "That's a complex issue, but how do you think we should approach it?" It's less about getting an answer and more about appearing deep and thoughtful. You're not clueless – you're contemplative!

Next, we have the 'Reflective Rebound.' This is for when someone asks you a question, and you, in a stroke of strategic genius, toss it back to them. "That's an interesting point, Mark. What are your thoughts on its implications?" Suddenly, you're not the deer in the headlights; you're Socrates leading a dialogue.

Don't forget the 'Strategic Stalling' technique. When asked something you have zero clues about, try, "That's a good question. Let's explore all the facets before jumping to conclusions." It's the boardroom equivalent of asking for directions without revealing you're lost.

In the world of leadership, asking questions isn't just about seeking answers; it's about showcasing your skill in navigating the unknown. It's about wearing the mask of wisdom, even if underneath, you're frantically flipping through mental files for a clue.

My fellow question-askers wield this secret weapon with pride. With every question you ask, you're not just avoiding revealing what you don't know; you're also giving the impression that you know a lot more than you do. In the grand theater of leadership, the one who asks the questions is often seen as the one holding the script.

Learning as a Leadership Style

Imagine a leadership style that doesn't demand you know everything but invites you to learn anything. Yes, even from the office cat (more on that later). Welcome to the world of Learning Leadership – it's less about being the smartest person in the room and more about being the most curious.

In this enlightened realm, every conversation is a classroom, every challenge a quiz, and every failure, well, let's call it an 'unexpected learning opportunity' (or a Tuesday). Here, the motto is "I have no idea what I'm doing, but I'm eager to learn!"

Let's take a page from the most underestimated guru in the office – the cat. Yes, you read that right. Ever watched a cat in a meeting? It sits, listens, occasionally naps, but when it acts, it's decisive. Be like the office cat: observe, ponder, and when the time is right, pounce (metaphorically speaking, of course).

I recall a leader, let's name her Linda. Linda had a habit of turning even coffee breaks into impromptu learning sessions. One day, she overheard two interns discussing Instagram strategies. Instead of strutting by with executive disdain, she pulled up a chair and asked, "Teach me your ways, oh wise ones." That day, Linda not only learned about hashtags but also earned the interns' undying respect.

Another time, a manager named Ron was faced with a tech problem that made the Apollo 13 crisis look like a hiccup. Instead of bluffing through it, Ron admitted, "I understand technology as much as I understand quantum physics, which is not at all." He then gathered a team of tech-savvy wizards and asked them to educate him. Not only did he solve the issue, but he also learned to tell his HTML from his HTTP.

Learning Leadership isn't about accumulating knowledge for the sake of it. It's about fostering a culture where curiosity is king, and 'I don't know' is the start of an adventure, not the end of an inquiry. It's a style where leaders are seen as explorers, armed with a compass of questions, mapping the unknown territories of challenges and opportunities.

So, embrace your inner learner. Ask, explore, and occasionally, take a lesson from the office cat – there's wisdom in those whiskers.

The Joy of Being Proven Wrong

In the grand opera of leadership, being proven wrong is not the tragic finale; it's more of a surprising plot twist that can lead to a standing ovation. Embrace the moment when someone waves the flag of correction, for it's not a white flag of surrender, but rather a colorful banner of enlightenment.

Picture yourself confidently striding into a meeting, armed with statistics and facts. You're delivering a presentation with the finesse of a seasoned Broadway star. Then, from the back of the room, a hand raises, and a voice gently points out that your data is, in fact, from a study about Antarctic penguin migration, not market trends. Oops.

There's an art to handling these moments, a finesse in turning a blunder into a graceful pirouette. The first step is the 'Elegant Pause' – that moment where you resist the urge to dive under the table and instead, take a breath and smile. It's like accidentally walking into the wrong restroom – just back away slowly and with dignity.

Next, we have the 'Gracious Pivot.' Instead of stubbornly defending your Antarctic penguin data, why not tip your hat to the corrector? Say something like, "Thank you for that insight! Just testing if you were all paying attention." It's not just saving face; it's acrobatic face-saving.

Then, there's the 'Reflective Rebound.' Turn the correction into a learning moment for everyone. "What a fascinating correction! Let's explore this further." Now, you're not just someone who was wrong; you're a sage who values growth.

Remember, being proven wrong is not an embarrassment; it's a luxury. It means you're surrounded by people who are not only smart but also brave enough to speak up. They're not your adversaries; they're your guides, leading you away from the land of misinformed decisions.

In the end, the joy of being proven wrong lies in the beautiful humanness of it. It keeps us grounded, reminds us we're fallible, and adds a dash of humility to our leadership recipe. After all, a leader who can laugh at their own mistakes is a leader who's as relatable as they are respected.

Embracing the Unknown

And now, dear leaders, let's draw the curtains on our first act with a rallying cry to embrace the great, vast unknown. Think of it not as a dark abyss of uncertainty, but as a theme park of possibilities – some rides might make you queasy, but oh, the thrill of the adventure!

Stepping into the unknown is like wearing a blindfold at a piñata party. Yes, you might miss a few swings (and accidentally hit a bystander), but the joy lies in the unpredictability and the chance of hitting that sweet spot.

Bid farewell to the burdensome belief that you must know everything. Release it like a balloon at a county fair and watch it float away into the sky of impossibility. In its place, welcome the liberating breeze of 'figuring it out as you go.' It's a breath of fresh air, infused with the scent of spontaneity and a hint of 'what on Earth am I doing?'

Imagine leading a team not with a map that claims 'X marks the spot,' but with a compass that says, 'North is probably this way, but let's find out together.' It's leadership as a journey, not a destination – more 'road trip with friends' and less 'guided tour with a strict itinerary.'

Embrace the unknown, and you embrace the essence of adventure in leadership. You'll find more joy in discovery, more excitement in innovation, and more stories to share (or embellish at dinner parties).

Gone are the days of the leader as the all-knowing oracle. Welcome to the era of the leader as the ever-curious explorer, armed with a quiver of questions and a shield of open-mindedness (and perhaps a snack for the road, because let's face it, adventures are hungry work).

Let's march, stumble, or skip forward into the unknown, with our flags of imperfection flying high. It promises a leadership experience that's not only more enjoyable but also less likely to result in a stress-induced need for a week-long retreat in a remote mountain cabin (though that does sound nice).

To lead is to learn – to embrace the unknown, to relish the unexpected, and to find joy in the journey. After all, the best stories come from the unplanned detours.

Chapter 2: Mistakes: The Unexpected Secret Weapon

Ode to the Oops

Gather round, leaders, and let's sing a song of praise to the unsung hero of the corporate world – the Mistake. Yes, those little (and sometimes not-so-little) blips, bloopers, and blunders that make HR cringe and give PR teams sleepless nights. In this ode to the oops, we celebrate the missteps, the miscalculations, and the 'what on Earth was I thinking' moments.

Let's visit a real-life blunder that serendipitously led to one of the most iconic office products in history. This is the tale of 3M's Post-it Notes, a story of accidental brilliance and a sticky situation turned gold.

Imagine Spencer Silver, a chemist at 3M, aiming to create a super-strong adhesive. What he ended up with was anything but. This adhesive was weak, hardly holding anything together – a seeming flop in the realm of stickiness. Enter Art Fry, a colleague of Silver's, who, plagued by his bookmarks constantly falling out of his hymnbook, saw potential in this 'failed' adhesive. He coated it on paper, and voilà – the bookmark stayed in place and could be repositioned without damaging the pages.

Initially, the idea didn't stick (pun intended) with 3M executives. It was a product in search of a problem, a solution waiting for its moment. But, undeterred, Fry pushed on. After a few modifications and a marketing campaign that included giving free samples to employees, the Post-it Note slowly gained traction.

Imagine the boardroom at 3M when the realization hit – their so-called blunder was turning into a blockbuster. The Post-it Note, born from a botched attempt at making a strong adhesive, was suddenly on every desk, in every office, and in every school. Spencer Silver's 'mistake' and Art Fry's vision transformed how we organize, plan, and remind ourselves of the mundane and the mighty.

The moral of this sticky story? Sometimes the best discoveries are hiding in plain sight, masquerading as failures. It's about looking at 'mistakes' not as dead ends, but as detours on the road to success. So, the next time you scribble a reminder on a Post-it, remember, it's more than just a piece of paper – it's a monument to the power of serendipitous mistakes.

Mistakes, dear friends, are the plot twists in our leadership narratives. They're not just stumbles; they're steps in a dance of discovery. They're not just errors; they're unexpected paths to innovation. In the world of leadership, the road to success is paved with good intentions and a few facepalm moments.

So, let's raise our coffee mugs to mistakes – those unpredictable, often embarrassing, yet wonderfully human experiences. They remind us that to err is not just human; it's a badge of honor in the ever-unpredictable journey of leadership.

More Famous Faux Pas

Let's explore some real-life examples where famed flubs turned into triumphant tales. These stories aren't just amusing anecdotes; they're beacons of hope for every leader who's ever thought, "Well, that didn't go as planned."

There is the serendipitous story of penicillin. Picture Alexander Fleming, a scientist whose lab cleanliness was, let's say, not exactly top-notch. Returning from a vacation, he found a moldy Petri dish that had killed the surrounding bacteria. Most of us would have reached for the disinfectant, but Fleming reached for the microscope. This 'oops' moment marked the birth of the world's first antibiotic, saving countless lives. It's a powerful reminder that sometimes, what you need is right there in your moldy dish – metaphorically speaking.

Don't forget the sweet slip-up of the chocolate chip cookie. Ruth Wakefield, running out of baker's chocolate, chopped up some semi-sweet chocolate, expecting it to melt into the batter. Instead, it held its shape, and voilà, the chocolate chip cookie was born. It's the kind of mistake that makes you say, "Thanks for not running to the store, Ruth."

And who could ignore the fizzy fortune of Coca-Cola? Originally concocted as a patent medicine by John Pemberton, this accidental beverage was initially marketed for its medicinal qualities. Little did Pemberton know, his syrupy mistake would fizz up to become one of the world's most popular soft drinks. Sometimes, the best recipes are the ones you didn't mean to make.

These real-life tales are more than just happy accidents; they're a playbook for the power of embracing the unexpected. They teach us that sometimes, the path to success is littered with mishaps, mix-ups, and 'maybe I shouldn't have done that.'

In the grand theater of leadership, remember: your next mistake might just be your biggest break. Keep your eyes open, and maybe don't clean your Petri dishes too often.

The Art of Graceful Stumbling

Welcome to the art of graceful stumbling, where every trip, slip, and tumble is not a dance with disaster, but a step towards serendipity. In the ballet of business, it's about turning a fall into a forward roll, a faux pas into a fancy pirouette. After all, if you're going to fall, why not make it fabulous?

Picture yourself navigating the tightrope of leadership. Below you are the pit of challenges, and you, armed with nothing but your wits and a questionable sense of balance. Now, when you inevitably stumble (because let's face it, who doesn't?), here are a few tips to do it with style:

- The Quick Recovery Quip: As you feel yourself losing balance, throw out a quip. "Just testing gravity, and yep, still works!" Humor is your parachute – it won't stop the fall, but it'll make for a more enjoyable descent.

- The Elegant Sidestep: When a project starts spiraling, don't panic. Do the elegant sidestep. Shift focus, pivot direction, and turn that stumble into a strategic stride. It's like dodging a puddle – only the puddle is a budget shortfall.

- The Philosophical Pause: If you trip over a challenge, pause and ponder. Stroke your chin, look thoughtful, and say something deeply philosophical like, "Ah, the complexity of it all!" It gives the impression that you're in deep contemplation, not deep trouble.

- The Laugh-It-Off Loop: When all else fails, laugh it off. Accidentally shared your vacation photos in the company-wide presentation? Chuckle and say, "And that's how not to do a presentation!" Laughter is the shock absorber of life's bumpy roads.

Remember, graceful stumbling isn't about avoiding mistakes; it's about embracing them with flair. It's about acknowledging that sometimes the path to success is littered with banana peels, and that's okay.

The next time you find yourself in a leadership stumble, remember these tips. Tuck, roll, and come up laughing. In the grand comedy of errors that is leadership, it's not about the fall – it's about the recovery, the grace, and the story you'll tell afterwards.

Mistakes as Learning Tools

In the secret playbook of leadership, every mistake is a chapter titled 'How Not to Do Things,' and believe me, it's a bestseller. These blunders, bloopers, and whoopsie-daisies aren't just mishaps; they're undercover training sessions for greatness, masquerading as moments we wish we could erase with a giant cosmic eraser.

Imagine each mistake as a wise, if slightly annoying, mentor. It taps you on the shoulder, clears its throat, and says, "Well, that didn't work, did it?" And just like that, you've been schooled in the art of 'let's try something different next time.'

Take, for instance, the time I confidently walked into a meeting and delivered an impassioned speech – only to realize I was in the wrong room, addressing a group of bewildered accountants. Not only did I learn to double-check room numbers, but I also discovered I could captivate an audience who knew nothing about the topic. Silver linings, my friends.

Then there was the team that decided to 'innovate' by changing their tried-and-true process, resulting in what can only be described as organized chaos. The lesson? If it ain't broke, maybe don't try to fix it with a sledgehammer. They didn't just learn about process optimization; they got a crash course in crisis management and team bonding.

And who could forget the marketing campaign that flopped harder than a belly flop at a diving competition? The team learned more about their audience in that one failure than in a year's worth of market research. It was like a masterclass in 'Understanding What Our Customers Don't Want.'

Each mistake is a steppingstone disguised as a stumble. They are the universe's way of saying, "Here's a lesson you didn't know you needed." It's experiential learning, with a side of humble pie.

Embrace your mistakes! Laugh at them, learn from them, and then tell their stories at parties. In the grand classroom of life, mistakes are the teachers we never asked for but definitely need. After all, the road to greatness is paved with facepalms and forehead slaps.

Now, here's a revolutionary idea: let's make mistakes a mandatory part of every brainstorming session. Think of it as the 'Blunder Brainstorm,' where the wilder and wackier your ideas, the better. It's like opening a Pandora's Box of creativity, but instead of unleashing evils, we're setting free a flurry of fantastically flawed concepts.

Imagine a meeting room where the usual phrase is not "That's a great idea!" but "What an epic blunder, let's explore it!" This is where 'bad' ideas come to shine, where the misfits of thought become the captains of innovation.

Picture this: A team sits around a table, throwing out ideas for a new product. Someone, let's call him Joe, suggests a solar-powered flashlight. Laughter echoes around the room. But then, the laughter fades into contemplative silence. "Wait a minute," says someone, "what if we use that concept for charging in daylight and working at night?" Suddenly, Joe's blunder becomes the seed for a new, eco-friendly invention.

Or consider the infamous case of a software team aiming to create an unbreakable encryption algorithm. By mistake, they create one so complex that even they can't figure it out. It's a facepalm moment until they realize they've accidentally invented the digital equivalent of an unsolvable puzzle – perfect for a new line of cybersecurity products.

And who can forget the advertising team trying to appeal to a younger audience? They mistakenly turn their serious brand mascot into a meme. Initially deemed a disaster, it unexpectedly resonates with the youth, sending brand popularity soaring. Their blunder didn't just create a buzz; it created a whole beehive of interest.

In the Blunder Brainstorm, it's all about flipping the script. Mistakes are not just tolerated; they're celebrated. It's a space where 'thinking outside the box' means setting the box on fire and seeing what shape the smoke makes. It's where the magic happens – in the chaotic cauldron of 'oops' and 'what ifs.'

So, next time you're brainstorming, invite mistakes to the party. Serve them a cocktail of curiosity and watch as they dance with ideas in a tango of innovation. Remember, some of the best ideas start as blunders – beautifully, wonderfully outrageous blunders.

Celebrating Screw-Ups

In the spirit of embracing our not-so-perfect journey, why not throw a party for our screw-ups? Yes, you heard right – it's time to celebrate our blunders, our missteps, and our glorious gaffes. Welcome to the world of 'Failure Parties' and 'Best Mistake of the Month' awards, where we toast to our errors because they often lead us to paths unknown and lessons invaluable.

Imagine walking into the office to find balloons and a banner that reads, "Congratulations on That Spectacular Mess-Up!" It's not about mocking the mistake; it's about celebrating the learning and the courage to try. These parties are where tales of slip-ups are shared, not with embarrassment, but with pride and a healthy dose of humor.

Let's start with the 'Best Mistake of the Month' award. Nominees are selected not for the gravity of their error, but for the creativity, learning, and innovation that sprung from it. Picture an award ceremony where Sarah, from accounting, wins for accidentally sending a payroll spreadsheet to the entire staff, inadvertently kickstarting a transparent conversation about salaries and equity. It's an "oops" that led to an "aha!"

Or how about 'Failure Parties'? These are events where teams gather to share their recent mistakes. There's Mike, who mixed up the client files and ended up presenting a business strategy to a bewildered yoga class. Then there's Linda, who forgot to mute herself during a virtual meeting and treated everyone to an impromptu karaoke session. The room erupts with laughter, not ridicule, because here, a faux pas is a badge of honor.

These celebrations serve a deeper purpose. They create a culture where risks are taken, innovation is born, and resilience is built. They remind us that the path to success isn't a straight line; it's more of a squiggle with occasional loops.

Why not celebrate the next time you or your team stumbles? Pop open a bottle of 'Bubbly Blunder' and raise a glass to the screw-up. After all, in a world that's obsessed with getting it right, a little celebration of getting it wrong can be incredibly right.

The Leader's Blooper Reel

Every leader has their own collection of bloopers, a highlight reel of moments they'd rather forget but absolutely shouldn't. It's like a comedy of errors, but the joke's on us. And trust me, I've had my share of laughable lapses.

There was the time I confidently walked into a crucial meeting, only to passionately argue points for the next week's agenda. It took me a good ten minutes (and several confused looks) to realize I was in the wrong week, both mentally and physically. In retrospect, it was a masterclass in how not to time travel.

Or the unforgettable episode where I, attempting to be hip and relatable, used what I thought was trendy slang during a presentation to our youngest team members. Let's just say, "Yeet" doesn't mean what I thought it meant, and my 'cool' factor plummeted faster than a lead balloon. It was a linguistic leap that ended in a linguistic faceplant.

And who could forget the virtual team retreat where I assured everyone that I was a pro at online tools, only to spend the first half-hour sharing my screen with a not-so-flattering view of my bewildered face and a backdrop of chaotic desktop icons. It was less 'tech-savvy executive' and more 'my dad just got his first computer.'

These bloopers, while cringe-worthy, are also invaluable. They're reminders that leadership isn't a sleek, polished performance; it's real, raw, and sometimes hilariously off-key. They teach us humility, keep us grounded, and provide ample material for team bonding (and gentle ribbing).

Cherish your blooper reel. Share your stories of mix-ups and misadventures. Laugh at them, learn from them, and let them remind you that perfection is overrated, but a good sense of humor is essential.

In the end, it's not the flawless moments that define us, but the flawed ones where we showed our humanity. Embrace your bloopers; wear them like badges of honor. After all, the best leaders aren't those who never falter, but those who can stumble, laugh, and get back up again.

Embracing Imperfection

As we wrap up this chapter on the symphony of stumbles that is leadership, let's take a moment to appreciate the beauty of imperfection. It's like a piece of abstract art – it might not make sense at first glance, but there's a profound beauty in its chaos.

Embracing imperfection in leadership is like learning to dance in the rain rather than waiting for the storm to pass. It's about making peace with the fact that you will sometimes step in puddles – and occasionally they'll be deeper than anticipated. But hey, that's what galoshes (and a good sense of humor) are for.

Think of your leadership journey as a well-loved novel. The best parts aren't the pristine pages; they're the dog-eared corners, the coffee stains, and the scribbled notes in the margins. They are the signs of a story well-read, a journey well-traveled.

As you march forward in your quest to guide, inspire, and innovate, remember to carry your mistakes with pride. Wear your blunders like medals earned in the battlefield of experience. Each misstep is a story, each gaffe a lesson, and each blooper a chance to grow.

Let's bid adieu to the quest for the unattainable perfection and welcome the wonderfully imperfect reality of leadership. After all, a spotless track record is not only unachievable; it's frankly a little suspicious.

Embrace your imperfections; they're what make you a genuine leader, not a leadership algorithm. They're the proof that you're human, approachable, and relatable. In a world obsessed with perfection, be a breath of fresh, unfiltered air.

In conclusion (yes, we're concluding without the transitional phrase), let your leadership journey be messy, vibrant, and authentically yours. Here's to the imperfections, the bloopers, and the beautiful chaos they bring. They don't just add character to your story; they are your story.

Chapter 3: The 'Good Enough' Leader's Survival Kit

Introduction to the Survival Kit

Welcome to the wilderness of 'Good Enough' Leadership, where every day feels like a cross between a jungle safari and a space expedition. In this uncharted territory, where the only predictable element is unpredictability itself, what you need is not a map to buried treasure, but a 'Good Enough Leader's Survival Kit.'

Imagine strapping on your boots for a trek through the dense underbrush of decision-making or donning a helmet for a voyage into the black hole of budget meetings. Here, the terrain is as varied as it is challenging, ranging from the Mountain of Misunderstandings to the Valley of Vague Feedback.

In these wilds, you won't encounter lions, tigers, or bears (oh my!), but you will face something far more bewildering: the ever-changing landscape of team dynamics, the mysterious fog of market trends, and the sudden sandstorms of unexpected project setbacks.

This is why the 'Good Enough Leader's Survival Kit' is essential. It's packed not with ropes and flares, but with tools more suited to the modern leader: a compass of common sense, a flashlight of flexibility, and perhaps the most critical of all, a sense of humor as your trusty sidekick.

So, fasten your seatbelt, adjust your compass, and prepare to embark on a thrilling adventure. With this survival kit in hand, you're not just ready to face the challenges of leadership; you're set to navigate them with a smirk, a wink, and an arsenal of good-enough strategies. Let the expedition begin!

The Cape of Humility

In the 'Good Enough Leader's Survival Kit,' the first and perhaps most dazzling item is the Cape of Humility. This isn't your ordinary superhero cape; it's woven from the finest threads of self-awareness and groundedness. When donned, it renders the leader invisibly humble, allowing them to glide through the corridors of power without tripping over the hem of an oversized ego.

The Cape of Humility is a remarkable garment. When worn, it miraculously shrinks any swelling of pride and inflates the often-deflated balloon of perspective. It's the perfect accessory for those moments when the applause is loud, and the accolades are many. It whispers gently, "Remember, you once accidentally screen-shared your vacation photos in a board meeting."

So, when should a leader wear this magical cape? Picture an employee feedback session. Here, the Cape of Humility transforms you from 'The Decider' to 'The Listener,' opening your ears and heart to what your team truly has to say. It's an essential attire for gracefully accepting critiques without the knee-jerk defense mechanisms kicking in.

Or consider the aftermath of a successful project. While it's tempting to bask in the glory, this is the perfect moment to don the cape. It helps you redirect the spotlight to your team, acknowledging their hard work and turning a personal victory into a collective celebration.

Remember, the Cape of Humility doesn't diminish your achievements; it enhances them. It ensures that your feet stay firmly on the ground, even when your head is in the clouds of success. So, wear it with pride – a humble, understated, yet incredibly stylish kind of pride.

Glasses for Hindsight Clarity

Next in our 'Good Enough Leader's Survival Kit' is an extraordinary pair of spectacles: the Glasses for Hindsight Clarity.

These aren't your average reading glasses; they are imbued with the magical ability to provide 20/20 vision in hindsight. They turn those 'should've, would've, could've' moments into crystal clear retrospections, perfect for learning from the past with the wisdom of a sage.

When you slip on these glasses, the blurred lessons of yesteryear come into sharp focus. That marketing campaign that flopped harder than a belly-flop contest? Through these lenses, you can see where the missteps happened and how to sidestep them in the future. It's like having a time machine, but instead of changing the past, you gain the wisdom to change the future.

Think of a time when you sent an office email that was as clear as mud, leading to a series of misunderstandings and a game of corporate telephone gone wrong. Put on these glasses, and suddenly, you see how a few well-placed words could have averted the chaos. It's like watching a replay of the big game, but you're both the coach and the quarterback.

These glasses are particularly handy when reviewing failed projects or initiatives. They remove the rose-tinted tint of nostalgia and the dark shades of regret, leaving you with a balanced view of what actually happened. With these glasses on, you can look back at the project not with a sense of failure, but with the understanding and insight necessary for future triumphs.

Whether you're sifting through the aftermath of a not-so-successful venture, or simply trying to understand where things went a bit awry, the Glasses for Hindsight Clarity are your go-to tool. Just remember, while they're great for learning from the past, don't forget to take them off and look forward to the future with unclouded eyes.

The Compass of Direction (Even When Lost)

Another indispensable item in our kit is the Compass of Direction (Even When Lost). This isn't your typical north-pointing navigator. Instead, it's a remarkable device that gives the illusion of unwavering direction and purpose, even when you're internally navigating the seas of confusion.

The beauty of this compass lies in its ability to make you appear as if you have an infallible sense of direction. You might not know whether you're heading toward a breakthrough or a breakdown, but to your team, you'll look like a leader with a plan, a purpose, and a path.

Imagine you're in a strategic meeting, and the discussion takes a turn into uncharted territory. You're as lost as a GPS with a dead battery, but fear not – a subtle glance at your Compass of Direction, and you're suddenly steering the conversation like a seasoned captain. It's the leadership equivalent of "fake it till you make it" – with a touch of magnetic magic.

Or picture a team-building exercise where you're expected to lead the way – literally. You have no clue left from right, but a quick peek at your compass, and you confidently guide your team through the metaphorical wilderness. It's about projecting confidence, even when your internal compass is doing loop-de-loops.

The key to using this compass effectively is subtlety. It's about those discreet glances, the slight nod of the head, the thoughtful pause – all giving the impression that you're consulting the stars of strategy, not the spinning arrow of guesswork.

In the end, the Compass of Direction (Even When Lost) is a reminder that sometimes, leadership is about projecting confidence while you quietly work out the details. It's a tool not just for finding the way but for reassuring others that there is a way to be found.

Inflatable Ego Raft

Tucked neatly in the 'Good Enough Leader's Survival Kit' is a unique, compact, and absolutely necessary item: the Inflatable Ego Raft. Designed for those days when the sea of criticism is choppy, and the waters of self-doubt are rising, this raft provides a temporary but essential buoyancy to your sagging spirits.

This isn't your typical pool float. It's an emergency device for those moments when your confidence is sinking faster than a lead balloon. The Inflatable Ego Raft is easy to deploy: simply pull it out, and recite your greatest hits – those past achievements, the kudos from colleagues, or that one time you nailed the impossible project. With each accolade, the raft puffs up, providing a comfortable cushion for your bruised ego.

Imagine you've just presented an idea in a meeting, and it lands with all the grace of a flying elephant. The room is silent, the feedback is tepid, and your confidence is quietly deflating under the table. That's when you reach for your Inflatable Ego Raft. Under your breath, you remind yourself, "I spearheaded last year's top project," and "I was employee of the month in June." Slowly but surely, your raft begins to inflate, lifting your spirits and your self-esteem out of the doldrums.

It's also perfect for those times when a project doesn't go as planned, and the whispers of self-doubt become a cacophony. A few minutes with your Inflatable Ego Raft, and you'll remember that failure is not a full stop, but a comma in the narrative of your leadership journey.

Of course, like any life-saving device, it's important to use the Inflatable Ego Raft responsibly. It's for temporary support, not permanent elevation. Use it to keep your head above water, but remember to deflate it once you're back on solid ground. After all, no one likes a leader who's permanently floating a few feet above reality.

So, the next time the waves of critique roll in, and your confidence feels like it's about to go under, remember your Inflatable Ego Raft. A few puffs of past praise and success, and you'll be riding the waves of leadership once again.

The Scepter of Delegation

Among the most prized items in the 'Good Enough Leader's Survival Kit' is the Scepter of Delegation. This isn't just a fancy stick; it's a symbol of the power and wisdom of delegating tasks – especially those that you'd rather slide off your desk and onto someone else's.

The Scepter of Delegation is imbued with the ancient art of knowing when to hold on and when to gracefully pass the baton (or in this case, the spreadsheet). It's for those moments when your to-do list looks like a never-ending scroll and your calendar is a mosaic of overlapping commitments.

Wielding the Scepter doesn't just lighten your workload; it's an exercise in trust and empowerment. Each time you delegate a task, you're not just saying, "I don't want to do this." You're saying, "I believe you can do this." It's an artful dance of giving responsibility while supporting from the sidelines.

Use the Scepter in tandem with magic phrases like "empowering team autonomy" or "fostering employee development." It's amazing how a task can transform from "something I dumped on you" to "an opportunity for growth and development." The scepter doesn't just pass tasks; it bestows opportunities.

Picture a team meeting where tasks are being distributed. With the Scepter of Delegation in your hand, you're not just assigning jobs; you're orchestrating a symphony of skills and talents. "John, you're excellent with numbers; take the lead on the budget analysis. Sarah, your creativity is unmatched; I'd like you to spearhead the design aspect."

Remember, the Scepter of Delegation is a tool of balance. It's about knowing when to lead from the front and when to guide from behind. Use it wisely, and watch as your team grows in confidence and capability, while you reclaim some much-needed space on your calendar.

So . . . the next time you feel overwhelmed, reach for the Scepter of Delegation. With a wave of this majestic rod, watch as tasks find new homes and your team discovers new strengths. After all, in the kingdom of leadership, a wise ruler knows when to delegate.

The Magic Mirror of Self-Reflection

Nestled within the 'Good Enough Leader's Survival Kit' is perhaps the most confronting yet enlightening tool: the Magic Mirror of Self-Reflection. Unlike the mirrors in fairy tales, this one doesn't show you the fairest of them all, but rather the raw, unvarnished truth of your own leadership style, complete with its flaws and foibles.

This isn't just any piece of reflective glass. When you gaze into this mirror, you're compelled to confront the parts of yourself that you often sweep under the rug of busyness and bravado. It's like having an honest conversation with yourself, minus the comforting delusions and ego-softening filters.

The Magic Mirror is particularly useful when you find yourself basking a bit too much in the glow of your own greatness. Feeling infallible? A quick look in this mirror will remind you of that time you accidentally replied all with a snarky comment. About to make grandiose promises? The mirror throws back a reflection of past pledges that fell into the abyss of overcommitment.

It's also an invaluable tool for personal growth. By forcing you to face your own shortcomings – be it a tendency to micromanage, avoid difficult conversations, or underappreciate your team – the mirror nudges you towards becoming a more effective and empathetic leader. It's like a personal coach, but without the motivational speeches and high fives.

When you look into the Magic Mirror of Self-Reflection, you might not always like what you see, but you'll certainly learn from it. It's about acknowledging that while you may not be perfect, you are a work in progress, and every glimpse in the mirror is a step towards improvement.

Before you stride into your next big decision or commit to another ambitious project, take a moment to peer into this mirror. It might just be the reality check you need to ensure your leadership is as effective as it is well-intentioned.

Emergency Parachute for Abrupt Exits

Tucked away for those special occasions in the 'Good Enough Leader's Survival Kit' is the Emergency Parachute for Abrupt Exits. This is not your average skydiving gear; it's designed for those moments in the boardroom or office when you need a quick and graceful escape from meetings that have gone south or conversations heading into a tailspin.

The Emergency Parachute is perfect for those times when a meeting morphs into a blame game, and everyone's looking at you for answers you don't have. Picture this: questions are flying, fingers are pointing, and the tension is thicker than the company handbook. That's your cue. You stand, deploy your parachute with a flourish of leadership panache, and gracefully exit the scene, leaving a trail of bewildered but impressed onlookers.

Operating the parachute is simple. At the first sign of a meeting turning into a quagmire – maybe the finance team starts throwing around terms like 'fiscal irresponsibility' – you subtly reach for your parachute. With a quick pull of the cord, it inflates, enveloping you in a cocoon of 'strategic withdrawal.' You're not running away; you're tactically regrouping.

This parachute is also ideal for those moments when you're asked a question that leaves you dumbfounded. Instead of mumbling a half-hearted response, activate your parachute. As it fills the room, use the ensuing confusion to make your exit, murmuring something about an urgent call or another meeting.

Of course, the use of the Emergency Parachute should be judicious. It's for those rare occasions when all other leadership tools have failed, and an escape is the only option. It's about knowing that sometimes, the most courageous thing a leader can do is make a strategic retreat and live to lead another day.

If you find yourself in a tight spot, with no clear way out, remember your Emergency Parachute. It's the perfect solution for when you need to bail out of a meeting gone awry – not just a lifesaver, but a sanity saver.

Toolkit of Patience and Perseverance

In the deeper recesses of the 'Good Enough Leader's Survival Kit' lies the indispensable Toolkit of Patience and Perseverance. This isn't your ordinary set of tools; it's a collection of satirical, yet symbolically significant, instruments designed for the long haul of leadership challenges.

First, we have the 'Hammer of Persistence.' This isn't for pounding nails but for driving home the commitment to long-term goals. When a project feels like running a marathon with a boulder strapped to your back, take out the Hammer of Persistence. With each swing, remind yourself and your team that every effort, no matter how small, is a step towards success. It's particularly effective when morale is low, and the finish line seems like a mirage.

Then there's the 'Screwdriver of Steadfastness.' This tool is perfect for those intricate problems that require a steady hand and a calm mind. When team conflicts arise or when the cogs of progress are stuck, use this screwdriver to gently, yet firmly, tighten the bonds of teamwork and loosen the screws of discord. It's about fine-tuning your approach to leadership, one twist at a time.

Don't overlook the 'Pliers of Patience.' These are essential for those moments when you need to hold onto your sanity while navigating the ups and downs of management. The Pliers of Patience are particularly useful when dealing with challenging team dynamics or navigating the labyrinth of organizational change. Grip onto your patience with these pliers, and no matter how slippery the situation, you won't lose your grasp.

Each tool in this kit comes with a set of humorous instructions. For example, "To use the Hammer of Persistence, swing with the rhythm of your favorite motivational anthem. Warning: overuse may lead to an overly optimistic outlook." Or, "The Screwdriver of Steadfastness is best used with a twist of humor and a turn of perspective. Caution: may cause an increase in team cohesion."

Whenever you're faced with a marathon project, a tangled conflict, or a test of your leadership mettle, reach for your Toolkit of Patience and Perseverance. It's the essential gear for building a foundation of resilience, project by project, challenge by challenge.

Assembling Your Kit

As we wrap up our expedition through the 'Good Enough Leader's Survival Kit,' let's talk about assembling your very own arsenal of leadership tools. Remember, this is less like putting together a piece of IKEA furniture (where there are always mysterious extra pieces) and more like packing for an adventure where the destination is as unpredictable as the weather.

Start by gathering your tools – both the tangible and the metaphorical. Place your Cape of Humility on a hanger for easy access; you never know when ego inflation might strike. Keep your Glasses for Hindsight Clarity polished; clarity often comes with a bit of hindsight smudge. And don't forget to periodically inflate your Ego Raft – just to ensure it hasn't developed any leaks from overuse.

Your Scepter of Delegation should be kept within arm's reach, preferably in a spot of honor on your desk. After all, delegation is a daily dance, and you're the choreographer. As for the Magic Mirror of Self-Reflection, give it a prominent place. A quick glance can often save you from a long fall.

And of course, let's not forget your Emergency Parachute for Abrupt Exits. While we hope you'll never need it, it's comforting to know it's there – just in case a meeting turns into a scene from a disaster movie.

The Toolkit of Patience and Perseverance should be regularly checked and restocked. Persistence can wear down even the sturdiest of tools, and patience, as we know, is often tested to its limits in the wilds of leadership.

Assemble your kit and remember, these tools are as much about attitude as they are about aptitude. They represent the qualities and traits that make the journey of leadership not just bearable, but enjoyable. Sure, there will be times when you wish you had a real parachute or an actual magic mirror, but part of the fun is improvising with what you have.

In conclusion, keep your survival kit close. It's your secret weapon in a world where being 'good enough' is not just acceptable, but commendable. Here's to the adventures ahead, the trails to be blazed, and the inevitable bloopers along the way – may your kit be ever handy, and your sense of humor ever ready.

Chapter 4: Delegation: Because Laziness Can Be Efficient

Welcome to Chapter 4, where we turn the table on laziness, dust it off, and polish it into a gleaming leadership strategy. In the world of good enough leadership, laziness isn't about doing less work; it's about doing less unnecessary work. It's about being smart with your sloth.

Let's redefine laziness. Here, it's a refined art form, a kind of strategic efficiency that separates the truly savvy leaders from the rest. Think of it as 'laziness with a purpose.' It's not about lounging on your office sofa binge-watching leadership webinars. It's about streamlining, prioritizing, and delegating tasks so that you can focus on what really matters – like finding that sofa in the first place.

The smartly lazy leader is a master of delegation. They view their to-do list not as a personal challenge, but as a buffet of opportunities for team development. Why hoard tasks when you can share the joy? It's like being a conductor of an orchestra; you don't need to play every instrument, just ensure that the music flows harmoniously.

These leaders understand that doing the least themselves doesn't mean work isn't getting done. It means work is being done more efficiently, more creatively, and probably with fewer sighs of exhaustion. They are the ones who look at a mountain of work and, instead of donning their superhero cape, hand out climbing gear to the whole team and map out the route together.

Let's toast to the smartly lazy leaders – the ones who have turned their desks into command centers of delegation and their calendars into masterpieces of minimalism. They are not just leaders; they are efficiency artists.

The Art of Strategic Delegation

Diving into the art of strategic delegation, let's explore how what some call laziness, the enlightened call a masterclass in efficiency. Delegating tasks isn't just about offloading work; it's about assigning it to those who can do it better, faster, or with a fresher perspective.

Think of yourself as the director of a play. You wouldn't try to act every part yourself, would you? Of course not. You'd cast the perfect person for each role. Similarly, strategic delegation involves identifying the strengths and capabilities of your team members and assigning tasks accordingly.

Here's how to delegate with finesse:

- The 'You've Got This' Technique: Instead of saying, "I don't have time for this," try, "You're the perfect person to handle this." It's about empowerment, not avoidance.

- The Art of Subtle Retreat: Once you've delegated, step back. Resist the urge to micromanage. It's like planting a seed; you need to give it space to grow, not pull it up every five minutes to check the roots.

And now, for some comical examples:

Done Right: Consider the time a manager turned a simple coffee order into a lesson in decision-making. "I trust your judgment," he said to the intern. The intern, empowered and eager, not only brought back coffee but also an assortment of pastries, turning a coffee run into an impromptu team celebration.

Done Wrong: Then there was the leader who asked his team to organize a crucial meeting but forgot to specify any details. The result? Three different meetings in three different places, none of which he attended because he was waiting in his office expecting a report. It was less delegation, more abdication.

Strategic delegation isn't about sitting back with your feet up (though that's a definite perk). It's about building a team that can function, flourish, and even surprise you, while you focus on the bigger picture – or your latte art skills. It's lazy, yes, but it's laziness done right.

Choosing the Right People for the Right Tasks

In strategic delegation, the key to success is assigning the right tasks to the right people. It's like casting a play – you wouldn't have your dramatic lead play the comic relief (unless you want some really awkward laughs). Here's a lighthearted look at using office personalities to your advantage and introducing the groundbreaking 'Lazy Efficiency Metrics.'

First, let's meet our cast of office characters:

1. The Eager Beaver: Always first to arrive and last to leave. Give them tasks that require enthusiasm and energy. Just don't assign them anything that requires a 'less is more' approach unless you want a simple task turned into a Broadway production.

2. The Zen Master: Calm under pressure, they're your go-to for crisis management. Don't, however, expect them to lead your pep rally. Their idea of excitement is a new type of herbal tea.

3. The Tech Whiz: They can solve any IT crisis with a few clicks, but they might not be the best choice for leading your public relations efforts unless you want all communication done via coding.

4. The Creative Soul: Brilliant for brainstorming and out-of-the-box thinking, but maybe don't rely on them for tasks requiring meticulous attention to detail. Last time, they turned a data entry task into an interpretive dance.

Now, onto the 'Lazy Efficiency Metrics.' This is a revolutionary tool for measuring how effectively you're delegating. It involves a complex algorithm of gut instinct mixed with keen observation, all while sipping your coffee.

Here's how it works:

- Task Matchup Score: How well does the task fit the person's skills? If you've got your Zen Master organizing the office party, something's gone awry.

- Enthusiasm Gauge: How excited are they about the task? If the Eager Beaver suddenly looks like a Sad Sloth, maybe reconsider your choice.

- Results Review: How well was the task executed? If the Tech Whiz's last project inadvertently crashed the server, maybe it's time to recalibrate.

Remember, strategic delegation using Lazy Efficiency Metrics isn't just about making your life easier (though that's a big plus). It's about optimizing your team's talents, balancing workloads, and maybe, just maybe, enjoying the sight of a well-oiled machine (even if you occasionally have to oil it yourself).

The Lazy Leader's Toolkit

In the adventurous journey of lazy-efficient leadership, having the right toolkit is crucial. This isn't your run-of-the-mill toolkit; it's a carefully curated collection of gadgets and gizmos that make delegation not just effective, but amusingly so. Let's unveil the contents of the Lazy Leader's Toolkit:

1. The Task Tossing Hat: A stylish fedora with a twist – it's perfect for those moments when you can't decide who to delegate to. Write down tasks on slips of paper, toss them into the hat, and let fate (or the nearest intern) decide. It's like playing leadership lottery, but with better odds.

2. Remote Delegation Darts: Ideal for the leader who prefers to delegate from a distance. Each dart is labeled with a different team member's name. Simply throw a dart at the provided board to assign tasks. Disclaimer: Not responsible for any ensuing office dart tournaments.

3. The Wheel of Delegation: Spin the wheel to assign tasks in a fun and entirely random manner. Each section of the wheel includes different team members and tasks. It's like a game show, but instead of winning a new car, you win a new project.

4. 'Not It' Nose Glasses: When a particularly unappealing task comes up, put on these glasses and declare "Not It." The task is then automatically passed to the next person. It's the adult version of the childhood game, but with more paperwork.

Each item in this toolkit comes with a tongue-in-cheek warning label: "Use with a sense of humor." After all, the art of delegation should be effective but can also be fun. So, go ahead and spin that wheel or toss that dart. Leadership just got a whole lot more entertaining.

Mastering the Art of 'Doing Nothing' Productively

In the hallowed halls of leadership, there's an ancient and mystical art that only the most enlightened leaders have mastered – the art of 'Doing Nothing' Productively. This paradoxical practice is not about lounging in your office hammock while chaos reigns outside (though that does sound appealing). It's about understanding that sometimes, the best action a leader can take is calculated inaction.

Imagine a leader, let's call him Bob, who perfected this art. Bob would often be seen staring contemplatively out of his office window, feet propped up, a picture of serene inactivity. Meanwhile, his team was busy being a whirlwind of productivity. Why? Because Bob's apparent inactivity wasn't laziness; it was strategic space-giving. His team didn't see an idle leader; they saw a leader who trusted them enough to let them fly solo. And fly they did, often to new heights of innovation and efficiency.

Then there was a CEO known among her peers as 'The Zen Master of Delegation.' She would calmly delegate tasks and then seemingly detach herself, adopting a hands-off approach that some mistook for idleness. In reality, she was giving her team the gift of autonomy and responsibility. The result? A team that felt empowered, capable, and remarkably productive.

This art is also about knowing when your involvement as a leader might be more of a hindrance than a help. It's the wisdom to recognize that stepping back can sometimes be the most powerful step forward. It's like being the director of a play who doesn't jump on stage to act but instead trusts the cast to deliver a stellar performance.

Remember, the next time you find yourself itching to jump into the fray, remember that there's strength in stillness, power in pause. By mastering the art of 'Doing Nothing' Productively, you're not just taking a break; you're breaking the mold of traditional leadership. It's about doing less so your team can do more – a leadership paradox that, when done right, can lead to unexpectedly successful outcomes.

Avoiding Over-Delegation: The Lazy Trap

There's a delicate dance between strategic delegation and just plain being a delegation diva. While we've sung praises of the art of doing less, there's a fine line between 'efficient laziness' and tumbling into the abyss of 'sheer sloth.' Welcome to the chapter on Avoiding Over-Delegation: The Lazy Trap.

Picture this: a leader, let's call him Dave, who took delegation so seriously that he once tried to delegate his coffee drinking. Dave's philosophy was, "Why do it yourself when someone else can?" That was all fun and games until his team started running the entire department while Dave became a professional email forwarder and meeting avoider.

Here are some laughable (yet alarmingly real) warning signs that you might be waltzing into the territory of over-delegation:

- Your Team Starts Sending You Meeting Invitations to Remind You What Your Job Is: When your team has to gently nudge you about your actual responsibilities, it's a sign. Maybe you've delegated a tad too much if your calendar is as empty as a politician's promises.

- You've Delegated Your Lunch Choices: If you find yourself asking your assistant whether you feel like a salad or sandwich today, pause and reflect. Next thing you know, you'll be delegating your chewing.

- You're Known More for Your Office Décor Than Your Contributions: When people start coming to your office more to see your exquisite collection of succulents rather than for leadership advice, it might be time to reassess.

The goal of delegation is to empower your team, not to create a miniature kingdom where you're the monarch of minimal effort. It's about striking a balance. Too little delegation and you're a micromanaging messiah; too much, and you're a leadership legend in your own lunchtime.

As you embrace the art of delegation, be wary of the siren song of over-delegation. It's all fun and games until someone ends up delegating their job right out of existence. Keep it smart, keep it balanced, and maybe keep an eye on your lunch choices.

Empowering Through Delegation

In the clever disguise of the 'lazy leader' lies a secret superhero of empowerment – the master of delegation. It's an art form that, under the guise of avoiding work, ingeniously leads to team growth and development. This chapter reveals how strategic delegation, often mistaken for a leader's clever ploy to dodge duties, can actually be a powerful tool for empowering employees.

Imagine a leader, let's call her Emma, who has perfected the art of delegation under the banner of 'efficient laziness.' Emma assigns tasks to her team not because she wants to avoid them, but because she sees the potential in each team member. It's like she's wearing x-ray glasses, seeing through the surface to identify hidden talents and opportunities for growth.

Here's the twist: While Emma enjoys her well-deserved downtime (perhaps perfecting the art of latte art or mastering sudoku), her team is thriving. The once timid intern is now leading meetings with confidence. The quiet coder in the corner is now brainstorming innovative solutions. Little do they know, Emma's 'laziness' is a carefully orchestrated plan to push them out of their comfort zones.

It's a win-win situation. The team gets opportunities to shine and develop new skills, while Emma gets to bask in the glory of a well-oiled machine (and an ever-growing collection of sudoku trophies). This approach may start as a way to lessen her load, but it inadvertently results in a stronger, more capable team.

What looks like a leader shirking responsibility is actually a leader cultivating a garden of talent. Each task delegated is a seed planted, which with the right guidance, grows into a forest of skills, confidence, and accomplishment.

While it may appear that Emma is just being her lazy self, she's actually employing one of the most effective methods of employee development. It's the ultimate leadership sleight of hand – or perhaps sleight of laziness – where avoiding work isn't just about relaxation; it's about elevation – of her team, their skills, and the entire workplace.

The Ethics of Lazy Leadership

In the realm of lazy leadership (yes, it's a realm), ethical considerations take center stage, albeit with a wry smile and a tongue-in-cheek attitude. The question arises: is it really ethical to be a lazy leader? Well, let's reframe that. It's not about shirking responsibilities; it's about redistributing them in a creatively empowering way. This isn't a tale of neglect, but one of clever redistribution and empowerment.

Imagine the ethical gymnastics here. Each task you delegate isn't just work off your plate; it's an opportunity on someone else's. It's not laziness; it's a disguised form of professional development. By stepping back, you allow others to step up. It's a beautiful cycle of growth, disguised as your desire to do less. Ethically speaking, you're practically a saint.

Let's weave through the ethical labyrinth with some mock-serious guidance. The Mirror Test is a great start. Each morning, assure your reflection that your avoidance of tasks is for the greater good. If you can say it without cracking a smile, you're mastering the art of ethical laziness.

Then there's the Empowerment Equation. With every task you offload, there's an unspoken promise of support and mentorship. It's not throwing someone into the deep end; it's more like providing them with swim lessons in a larger pool. It's an equilibrium of giving and guiding.

Remember, there's a fine line between being a strategic delegator and turning into part of the office scenery. Regular self-checks are crucial. Are you a pillar of delegation wisdom or just a decorative column? Striking this balance is key.

The ethics of lazy leadership hinge on the motive behind the minimalist approach. It's being smart and strategic rather than simply slothful. When practiced with care and cunning, lazy leadership transcends ethical dilemmas and becomes a badge of clever and caring management. So embrace your lazy leadership – ethically, responsibly, and with a clever twist.
Embracing Your Inner Lazy Leader

As we bring the curtains down on this exploration of lazy leadership, it's time for a rousing, albeit laid-back, call-to-action. Leaders of the world, it's time to embrace your inner lazy leader. Yes, you heard that right. In the paradoxical universe of leadership, sometimes the most effective action is, well, a masterfully crafted inaction.

Let's paint a picture here: envision a leader who has mastered the art of doing less but achieving more. This leader isn't sprawled on a couch all day, tossing tasks at people like confetti. No, this is a leader who has fine-tuned the skill of strategic delegation, who knows that empowering a team isn't just about giving them tasks, but about giving them wings. This leader understands that their apparent inactivity isn't a sign of disinterest, but a sign of trust and confidence in their team.

If you find yourself feeling guilty about not being a whirlwind of constant activity, relax. Sometimes, the whirlwind needs to take a break and turn into a gentle breeze. Remember, a lazy leader isn't necessarily an ineffective leader. In fact, they could be the most effective leader of all, spinning their web of efficiency from the shadows (or possibly from a hammock).

Don't be afraid to embrace your inner lazy leader. It's about being efficient in your laziness and purposeful in your delegation. It's about understanding that sometimes, the best thing you can do is take a step back and let others step forward. So, go ahead, lean back in your chair, prop your feet up, and watch as your team astonishes you with their capabilities. After all, in the grand theater of leadership, sometimes the best action you can take is a well-planned and well-deserved moment of inaction.

Chapter 5: Feedback: How to Smile While Being Criticized

The Art of the Nod: Mastering Body Language

Welcome to the art of the nod, an essential skill in the 'Good Enough Leader's' repertoire, especially when navigating the treacherous waters of feedback. Let's face it, receiving criticism can feel like being in the splash zone of a verbal water park. But fear not, for with the right body language, you can transform this experience from a drenching downpour into a refreshing mist.

First up, the nod. This isn't just any nod; it's a carefully calibrated movement that says, "I'm listening, I'm understanding, and no, I'm not plotting your immediate transfer to the Antarctic office." The key is in the frequency and amplitude. Too slow, and you risk appearing disinterested; too vigorous, and you might come off as a bobblehead. Aim for a serene, wise nod – think of it as channeling your inner sage who has seen it all and remains unfazed.

Eye contact is your next tool. It's a delicate balance between maintaining a steady gaze and not staring into the soul of your critic like a hungry owl. The trick is to look interested but not intense. Remember, you're receiving feedback, not engaging in a telepathic battle.

And then, the unwavering smile. This isn't a grin or a smirk; it's a polite, "I'm receptive to your words" smile. It's the facial equivalent of a diplomatic handshake. This smile should say, "Thank you for your feedback," not, "Wait till you see your next performance review."

Now, picture this exaggerated scenario: You're receiving feedback, and instead of the artful nod, you go for a full headshake. Your eye contact is more laser beam than gentle gaze. And your smile? It's a cross between a grimace and a forced grin seen in awkward family photos. The result? A feedback session that's more uncomfortable than sitting on a whoopee cushion at a board meeting.

On the flip side, imagine employing the art of the nod perfectly. Your head moves with the grace of a metronome, your eyes convey understanding and appreciation, and your smile is the epitome of gracious acceptance. Here, you're not just listening; you're demonstrating the poise and composure of a leader who can take feedback and still look like they're ready for a magazine cover.

So, as you face the firing squad of feedback, remember: nod wisely, gaze kindly, and smile diplomatically. It's not just about surviving criticism; it's about thriving in it, one nod at a time.

Translating Criticism into Compliments

One of the most critical acts is learning to translate criticism into compliments. It's like being a linguistic alchemist, turning the lead of negative feedback into the gold of positive affirmations. This skill isn't just about preserving your ego; it's about finding the silver lining in every cloudy comment.

Let's dive into some playful translations. When someone says, "This is totally wrong," what they're really saying is, "Thank you for recognizing my creative approach!" It's a matter of perspective. Your idea wasn't off-base; it was so innovative that it circled back to base.

Consider the feedback, "This report is a complete mess." Ah, what they mean to say is, "I admire your non-traditional structure and unique organizational style." It's not chaos; it's revolutionary formatting.

Now, picture this hypothetical scenario: A leader, let's call him Ted, receives feedback that his presentation was "confusing and erratic." Ted, a master translator, puffs up with pride and responds, "Thank you for acknowledging my ability to think outside the box and keep the audience guessing!" The confused looks from his team only confirm his belief that they are in awe of his avant-garde methods.

Or imagine a leader who interprets "Your management style is intimidating" as "Your charismatic leadership commands the room!" Suddenly, what was a critique becomes a testament to their powerful presence.

Of course, there's a fine line between translation and delusion. It's important to extract the constructive elements from feedback rather than completely repaint the picture. But in the moment, a little mental translation can be the spoonful of sugar that helps the medicine go down.

The next time you're on the receiving end of less-than-glowing feedback, put on your translator hat. Each critique is an opportunity to hear a compliment in disguise, an affirmation waiting to be unveiled. It's not just about making yourself feel better; it's about reinterpreting the message in a way that empowers rather than disheartens. After all, in the world of leadership, every piece of feedback is just a misunderstood compliment in waiting.

The 'Thank You' Reflex

In the grand performance of receiving feedback, one of the most pivotal moves is the 'Thank You' Reflex. It's a simple, yet profound response: no matter the content, nature, or tone of the feedback, your first words should always be, "Thank you." This isn't just good manners; it's strategic graciousness. It's about acknowledging the feedback giver, even if their words feel more like a roast at a comedy club than a constructive review.

Picture this: You've just been told, "Your project plan looks like it was made by a four-year-old." Instead of reacting with defensiveness or a well-aimed paper airplane, you respond with a serene, "Thank you." It's disarming, unexpected, and sets the stage for a more productive conversation. Plus, it gives you time to compose yourself and not blurt out what you're really thinking.

Let's explore some satirical examples. Imagine someone says, "This is the worst idea I've heard in my entire career." With the 'Thank You' Reflex, you respond, "Thank you for your honesty and for setting a new benchmark for my ideas." It's a reply that's coated in a thick layer of gratitude and just a hint of sarcasm.

Or consider a scenario where the feedback is, "Your presentation skills are... interesting." Here, the 'Thank You' Reflex comes to your rescue. "Thank you for finding my presentation style noteworthy," you say, with a smile that hides your bewilderment.

The beauty of the 'Thank You' Reflex is that it buys you time and maintains your composure. It's like a verbal judo move, where you use the momentum of the critique to maintain balance and poise. It doesn't mean you agree with the feedback; it means you're wise enough to acknowledge it gracefully.

Embrace the 'Thank You' Reflex. Make it an automatic part of your feedback arsenal. It's not just about being polite; it's about being tactfully resilient. Whether the feedback is a gentle nudge or a full-blown shove, a heartfelt 'thank you' is your first line of diplomatic defense.

Creating a Feedback Absorber Shield

In the adventurous journey of leadership, amid the slings and arrows of outrageous feedback, there exists a secret weapon: the imaginary 'Feedback Absorber Shield.' This isn't your average medieval armor; it's a modern, mental gadget designed to protect not just your ego, but also your morale. It's for those times when feedback feels like a hailstorm of negativity, and you need something to prevent a complete washout.

Imagine this shield as a personal force field, invisible yet invincible. As soon as the first drops of critical feedback begin to fall, you activate your shield. It doesn't just deflect the negative emotions; it transforms them into something constructive. Think of it as an alchemist's stone for feedback, turning the lead of criticism into the gold of growth.

Here's how it works: When someone says, "Your approach is completely wrong," your shield kicks into action. Instead of letting that comment bruise your ego, the shield filters it, and you hear, "Here's an opportunity to explore new approaches." It's like having a translator that rephrases every blow into a pat on the back.

Consider it in action: You're in a meeting, and the feedback is coming in fast – not all of it gentle. With your Feedback Absorber Shield up, the comments bounce off, leaving behind nuggets of wisdom instead of dents of despair. "This project is a disaster," turns into, "This project is a learning experience." "You're not leading effectively," becomes, "You're leading with room for improvement."

This shield is especially useful when the feedback is less about constructive criticism and more about venting frustration. It allows you to stay calm, collected, and focused on the valuable insights hidden in the barrage of comments. It's not about ignoring the feedback; it's about reframing it into something you can use to fortify, not just your leadership skills, but also your mental well-being.

Remember your Feedback Absorber Shield the next time you brace for a feedback session. With it, you can turn even the harshest critique into a chance to learn, grow, and prove that in the world of leadership, the best defense is a good reframe.

Feedback Bingo: Turning Pain into a Game

In the whimsical world of leadership, who says feedback sessions can't be a bit of fun? Enter 'Feedback Bingo,' a game that transforms the often-dreaded feedback process into an amusing, almost enjoyable activity. This isn't your grandma's Bingo; it's a leader's guide to turning pain points into points of play.

Here's the gist: You create a Bingo card, but instead of numbers, each square contains a common critique phrase. "Needs more initiative," "Too hands-off," "Can improve on time management" – these are your Bingo squares. As you sit through your feedback session, each time a phrase on your card gets mentioned, you get to check off a square. The goal? Aim for a full house and turn those critiques into a triumphant shout of "Bingo!" – internally, of course.

Let's paint a picture of Feedback Bingo in action. You walk into your feedback session, armed not with defensiveness, but with your Bingo card, mentally prepared. As the session unfolds and phrases get thrown around, you mentally tick off squares. "Lacks strategic thinking" – check. "Overly enthusiastic in meetings" – check. It's almost disappointing when a comment doesn't match your card.

The beauty of Feedback Bingo lies in its ability to lighten the mood – in your mind, at least. Each check on the card is a small victory, a way to gamify the sting of criticism. It's not about dismissing the feedback; it's about reframing it into a challenge. Can you get a full house? Can you predict the feedback so well that your Bingo card is a pre-emptive strike against surprise? Of course, this game comes with a wink and a nudge. It's a mental exercise in humor, a way to bring a little lightness to a process that can sometimes feel heavy. By the end of the session, even if you don't achieve a full house, you'll likely find that the feedback was easier to digest when you turned it into a game.

The next time you brace for a feedback session, consider playing a round of Feedback Bingo. It's a unique way to transform a potentially painful process into an amusing game. Who knows, you might just find yourself looking forward to your next feedback session – Bingo card in hand.

The Compliment Sandwich: Feeding Criticism to Others

In the culinary art of feedback, one dish reigns supreme: the Compliment Sandwich. This is a delicacy in the world of leadership, where criticism is nestled between two thick slices of praise. But in the hands of a 'Good Enough Leader,' this isn't just any sandwich – it's a gourmet experience with compliments so lavish, they could be mistaken for royal decrees, and criticism so subtly placed, it's like a whisper in a hurricane.

Let's break down the recipe for this extravagant Compliment Sandwich. Start with the first slice of bread – a compliment so grandiose, it could inflate a hot air balloon. "Your creativity shines brighter than the sun in a cloudless sky," is an excellent opener. It sets the stage and ensures the recipient is basking in the glow of admiration. Next, the filling – the criticism, but make it as gentle as a feather landing on a pillow. "However, your reports could be a tad more punctual," you might say, with the lightest touch. It's criticism, yes, but delivered in a tone that's softer than a lullaby.

Finally, top it off with the second slice of bread – another outlandishly grand compliment. "Your dedication to this job is the stuff of legend, echoing through the halls of time," you declare. This isn't just a compliment; it's an epic poem of praise.

Here's an example of an outrageously over-the-top Compliment Sandwich in action: "Your brilliance in meetings is blinding, like a beacon of wisdom guiding us through the fog of uncertainty. It would be an added boon to the cosmos if your email responses were slightly more expedient. Nevertheless, your work ethic is a marvel, a tireless wonder rivaling the ceaseless waves of the ocean."

The beauty of the Compliment Sandwich is its ability to deliver feedback in a way that's palatable, even delightful. It's about cushioning the blow with such extravagant praise that the recipient might just forget there was any criticism at all.

When it's time to serve up some feedback, remember the Compliment Sandwich. Make it hearty, make it extravagant, and most importantly, make it memorable. After all, in the world of feedback, it's not just what you say; it's how you garnish it.

Deciphering the Code: What They Really Mean

Navigating the labyrinth of feedback often feels like trying to decipher an ancient code. Beneath the polite veneers of certain phrases, there lie hidden meanings, waiting to be unraveled by the astute leader. Welcome to "Deciphering the Code: What They Really Mean," where we translate common feedback phrases from 'Corporate Speak' to plain English. Let's dive into our glossary of feedback translations:

1. "That's an interesting idea." Translation: "That idea is so bizarre; it belongs in a science fiction novel. But I'm too polite to say it outright."

2. "We appreciate your unique approach." Ah, this one means, "You've completely ignored the brief, but at least you're creative."

3. "Let's circle back on this." The age-old code for "This discussion is going nowhere fast, and I'd rather revisit it when I've had enough coffee to cope."

4. "You bring a lot of energy to the team." Often translates to, "You talk more than anyone I've ever met, and I'm not sure it's all productive."

5. "You're a real team player." Sometimes this means, "You're great at agreeing with everyone, even if we're all agreeing to jump off a cliff."

6. "I love your enthusiasm." A polite way of saying, "Your ideas are a little too wild, but at least you're passionate."

7. "Could you take more initiative?" This one's code for "Why do I always have to tell you what to do? Can't you just read my mind already?"

8. "You have a lot of potentials." Translated, it means "You haven't quite got the hang of this yet, but I'm hopeful you're not a lost cause."

9. "This needs some more polish." A kind way of saying, "Start over. This time, maybe actually use the guidelines I provided."

10. "I'm not sure this aligns with our vision." This means, "This is the opposite of what we want, but I don't want to crush your spirit."

Remember, these translations are offered with a wink and a nudge. It's about finding humor in the nuances of feedback and learning to read between the lines. By deciphering these codes, you not only become a connoisseur of corporate linguistics but also gain insights into what's truly being said – a valuable skill for any leader. There might just be a hidden message waiting to be decoded, and with this guide, you're well-equipped to crack the code.

Embracing the Feedback Frenzy

As we reach the end of our journey through the wild world of feedback, it's time to embrace the Feedback Frenzy. Yes, even the scathing, soul-crushing type. After all, feedback, in all its forms, is a crucial ingredient in the recipe for growth and development. But remember, the secret spice is a sense of humor.

Imagine facing the tornado of feedback not as a hapless bystander but as a seasoned storm chaser. Each critique, no matter how sharp, is a gust of wind pushing you towards becoming a better, more resilient leader. Sure, the ride might be bumpy, and you might get a little queasy, but the destination – a place of improved insight and understanding – is worth it.

Yet, facing this frenzy doesn't mean losing your sense of humor. Laugh at the absurdity, smile at the over-the-top critiques, and nod sagely at the contradictions. Feedback might be serious business, but it doesn't have to be solemn. It's like being in a comedy-drama – the situation is intense, but there's always room for a chuckle.

In summary, the world of feedback is an untamed beast, but one that you, as a leader, are fully equipped to tame. Embrace each piece of feedback with the grace of a diplomat and the grit of a warrior. Remember, every 'interesting idea' and every 'unique approach' is a steppingstone on your path to greatness.

If you are in the line of feedback fire, face it with a smile, a nod, and maybe a hidden Bingo card in your pocket. After all, in the grand theatre of leadership, feedback isn't just an act; it's the whole play, and you're the star.

Embracing feedback is akin to being a culinary critic in the diverse restaurant of leadership. You're going to taste some dishes that are less than palatable, but each bite, no matter how bitter, has its own value. Approach this smorgasbord of opinions with a grin, a pinch of salt, and the knowledge that every morsel of criticism adds flavor to your leadership journey. Remember, the key to digesting feedback is not just a strong stomach, but a resilient sense of humor. So, when the next course of critiques is served, be ready with your fork of wit and your knife of perspective – it's time to feast on feedback with a smile!

Chapter 6: The Fine Art of Mediocre Decision Making

Introduction to Mediocre Decision Making

Welcome to the world where perfect decision-making is dethroned, and mediocrity is celebrated with a confetti cannon of common sense. In this chapter, we dive into the Fine Art of Mediocre Decision Making, an area often overshadowed by the relentless pursuit of perfection in leadership circles.

Let's face it: the pressure to make flawless decisions is like trying to cook a gourmet meal when you've only ever mastered cereal. It's time to challenge this over-glorification of perfection. After all, isn't life itself a series of gloriously imperfect choices?

Here's a toast to the mediocre decision – the unsung hero in a world obsessed with getting it right all the time. These are the decisions that keep the wheels turning, albeit sometimes with a bit of a squeak. They're not the choices that will catapult you into the annals of leadership legends, but they'll keep you safely away from the blooper reels of disastrous decisions. In this light-hearted exploration, we'll argue that sometimes the best decision is a wonderfully average one. It's the middle ground, the safe bet, the "let's not rock the boat but maybe give it a gentle nudge." It's about finding beauty in the beige, the magnificence in the mundane.

Buckle up for a ride through the middle lane of decision-making. It's not going to be a rollercoaster of extreme highs and lows. Instead, expect a pleasant drive through the scenic route of satisfactory choices and good-enough outcomes. After all, in the relay race of leadership, sometimes it's okay to be the runner who keeps a steady pace, rather than sprinting for glory or tripping over ambition.

Celebrating the 'Meh'

In the grand opera of leadership, there's a special kind of aria sung for decisions that are gloriously, unabashedly 'meh.' These are the choices that don't send ripples through the cosmos but do keep the boat steady and afloat. Let's celebrate the beauty and relief of decisions that are just "good enough."

Picture the scene: You're faced with a decision. The options are many, the stakes are medium, and the coffee is lukewarm. You weigh the pros and cons, you tally the risks and rewards, and then you choose the path of least resistance – the middle road, the safe bet, the 'good enough' option. It's not going to make headlines, but it also won't cause sleepless nights. It's the decision-making equivalent of a comfortable pair of shoes – not flashy, but they get you where you need to go. Now, let's look at some famous 'meh' decisions that turned out surprisingly well. Consider the executive who decided to market a failed adhesive as a low-tack, repositionable note – and thus, the Post-it Note was born, an icon of office mediocrity that somehow revolutionized how we remember things. Or the TV producer who chose to air a show about nothing, filled with mundane conversations and everyday occurrences. That show? "Seinfeld." It was a shrug of a decision that led to one of the most successful sitcoms in history.

These examples show that sometimes, the best choice is the lukewarm one. It's about recognizing that not every decision needs to be a leap across a chasm of uncertainty. Sometimes, a small step, a 'meh' choice, is all it takes to move forward.

In the world where every decision feels like it must be groundbreaking, there's a certain charm in embracing the 'meh.' It's a reminder that sometimes, good enough really is good enough, and that there's a certain grace in the art of the average.

The Half-Baked Decision Spectrum

In the culinary world of leadership, there exists a unique measuring tool: the 'Half-Baked Decision Spectrum.' This satirical instrument is designed to gauge the doneness of your decisions, ranging from slightly undercooked to barely seeing the inside of an oven. Let's embark on a tongue-in-cheek exploration of the various levels of decision-making mediocrity.

At one end of the spectrum, we have the "Slightly Doughy" decisions. These are the choices that have a solid foundation but lack a crisp edge. Think of them like a cookie that's chewy in the middle – not quite fully formed, but palatable. These decisions are made with some information and a sprinkle of gut feeling. They're the 'safe bets' in the decision-making world.

Moving along the spectrum, we encounter the "Halfway There" decisions. These are akin to a pie that's golden on the edges but still jiggly in the center. These choices are made with more hope than certainty, a dash of data, and a generous helping of wishful thinking. They might work out, or they might leave you with a bit of a mess – it's a culinary gamble.

Next up is the "Just Warmed Up" level. Here, decisions are akin to a casserole that's been in the oven just long enough to be lukewarm. Made with minimal information and a hefty dose of 'it'll probably be fine,' these choices are the shrugs of the decision-making process. They're not going to win any awards, but they probably won't cause any disasters either.

Finally, at the far end of the spectrum, we have the "Barely in the Oven" decisions. These are the wild guesses, the shots in the dark, the 'let's just see what happens' choices. They're like throwing ingredients in a pot and hoping it turns into soup. Sometimes, you'll be pleasantly surprised. Other times, well, let's just say it's a learning experience.

The Half-Baked Decision Spectrum serves as a humorous guide to the different levels of decision mediocrity. It's a reminder that not every decision needs to be perfectly cooked to be effective. Sometimes, a half-baked choice can lead to a full-course success – or at least a memorable snack.

Advantages of Not Trying Too Hard

In the comically unpredictable world of leadership, a little-known secret weapon lies in not sweating every decision. We call it the 'Meh Method' – a strategic embrace of the good enough. Let's dive into this with a chuckle, guided by real-life examples that prove sometimes, the most brilliantly effective decisions are those that are just... fine.

Consider the stress-busting joy of mediocrity. There's a delightful ease in saying, "That'll do," and moving on. It's like choosing to wear mismatched socks because, really, who's going to notice? Leaders who adopt this laid-back approach find themselves less in a tizzy and more in a Zen-like state of calm. After all, not every decision needs to be a Shakespearean drama.

Then there's the time-saving magic of the 'Meh Method.' Why spend hours agonizing over the perfect choice when a perfectly adequate one will suffice? It's the leadership equivalent of choosing the shortest grocery line – you may end up behind someone with a year's supply of canned beans, but hey, at least you're moving.

Now, let's chuckle over some real examples:

- Southwest Airlines' Quick Turnaround: Southwest Airlines decided their planes would spend less time lounging around airports and more time in the air. It wasn't rocket science, just common sense with a side of efficiency. This 'meh' decision skyrocketed their profits and had other airlines scratching their heads and wondering why they didn't think of something so brilliantly basic.
- IKEA's Flat-Pack Revolution: When IKEA chose to flat-pack their furniture, it wasn't because they were visionaries; they just wanted to fit more stuff in a truck. This decision, possibly made over a coffee break, turned out to be a game-changer. Suddenly, people worldwide were happily cursing in Swedish while assembling their furniture, all thanks to a decision that was more about convenience than genius.

These examples show that a dash of mediocrity can lead to extraordinary results. So, the next time you're facing a decision, remember aiming for the stars is great, but sometimes shooting for the streetlamp and hitting it is just as impressive. Embrace the 'Meh Method,' and who knows? You might just stumble upon your own version of flat-pack success or quick-turnaround triumph.

Tools for Mediocre Decision Making

In the whimsical world of 'Good Enough' leadership, the tool belt of a mediocre decision-maker is filled with gadgets that are as comically unscientific as they are unexpectedly effective. Let's explore some of these tongue-in-cheek tools and methods, designed to elevate your decision-making to new heights of mediocrity.

First up is the 'Magic 8-Ball of Indecision.' Perfect for those moments when making a decision feels like solving a Rubik's Cube blindfolded. Just give it a shake and let the universe decide. "Should we expand into new markets?" Shake, shake, shake – "Reply hazy, try again." Ah, the comforting embrace of indecision!

Next, we have the 'Dartboard of Destiny.' This isn't just any dartboard; it's your strategic guide to randomness. Pin your options to the board, grab a dart, and let fate take the wheel. It's like choosing your dinner venue by throwing a spaghetti noodle at a map. Who knew strategy could be this much fun?

Then there's the 'Wheel of Whimsy.' Spin the wheel to make your next big decision. Each section represents a different choice, from "Yes, immediately" to "Ask the intern." It's decision-making meets game show – excitement and unpredictability in every spin!

Don't forget the 'Coin Flip of Courage.' A simple, classic, and surprisingly effective method for when you're torn between two options. Heads, we do it; tails, we don't. It's decision-making stripped down to its underwear – bold and a little bit reckless.

For the more digitally inclined, there's the 'App of Ambiguity.' It's like a dating app, but for decisions. Swipe left, swipe right, and find your mediocre match. Perfect for those who like a bit of tech in their indecision.

As for when and how to use these tools, the key is a blend of humor and a willingness to embrace the absurd. They're ideal for decisions that won't trigger an apocalypse if they go sideways. Use them to inject a bit of levity into the process, to remind yourself that not every decision is life-or-death – some are just life-or-lunch.

In conclusion, the toolkit for mediocre decision-making is about balancing fun with function. It's a celebration of the less serious side of leadership, where the journey of decision-making is sprinkled with laughter, randomness, and a healthy dose of "let's just see what happens."

The Art of Indecision

In the gallery of leadership tactics, there hangs an often-overlooked masterpiece: the Art of Indecision. Contrary to popular belief, this isn't about being wishy-washy. It's a calculated strategy, where sometimes the shrewdest move is to not move at all. Let's explore the subtle genius of choosing, well, not to choose.

Imagine leadership as a game of chess, but with a twist: sometimes the best move is to just stare at the board, ponder, and then go make a cup of tea. It's not about rushing to action; it's about embracing the power of the pause, the might of the maybe.

Now, let's delve into some humorous strategies for effectively postponing decisions:

- The Calendar Shuffle: When faced with a decision, solemnly consult your calendar, furrow your brow, and then declare, "I need to find the right time to think about this." It's a masterful blend of appearing busy while buying yourself some decision-free peace.

- Consulting the Oracle: Announce that you need to consult with various experts, advisors, or even your pet cat before making a decision. It's a great way to defer the choice while giving the impression of seeking wise counsel. "I can't decide this until Mr. Whiskers weighs in," you say, with a straight face.

- The Perpetual Pilot: Suggest starting a pilot project for every decision. It's like dipping your toes in the pool without committing to a swim. "Let's pilot this idea of changing our email font and revisit in six months," you propose, knowing full well that fonts are a deeply complex matter.

- The Meeting Marathon: Propose a series of meetings to discuss the decision, stretching so far into the future that everyone forgets what the decision was about. It's the corporate equivalent of kicking the can down the road, then forgetting where the road is.

- The Philosophical Approach: Whenever a decision looms, turn philosophical. Ponder the nature of choice, the illusion of free will, the butterfly effect. By the time you're done, people are too confused to remember there was a decision to be made.

The Art of Indecision isn't about avoiding responsibility; it's about recognizing that sometimes the best decision is to let the decision marinate a bit. It's about understanding that not every crossroad requires an immediate turn. Sometimes, standing at the crossroad, admiring the scenery, and pondering the meaning of the road is the wisest journey of all.

Mediocre Decision Making in Action

In the intriguing world of leadership, there's a certain flair to making wonderfully mediocre decisions. Let's explore some exaggerated case studies of leaders who embraced this with gusto, diving into how their so-so choices played out – for better or for worse – and the laughably insightful 'lessons learned' from each.

Case Study 1: The CEO Who Chose the Office Color Based on Her Cat's Fur

Meet CEO Linda, who had to decide on a new color scheme for the office. Overwhelmed by choices, she glanced at her cat, Whiskers, and declared, "Let's go with his fur color – it's neutral enough." The result? An office awash in a unique shade of tabby that surprisingly boosted morale, as it reminded everyone of adorable kittens. Lesson learned: Sometimes the best inspiration is sitting on your lap, purring.

Case Study 2: The Manager Who Solved Scheduling Conflicts with a Magic 8-Ball

Kevin, a manager, faced a team scheduling nightmare. With a shrug, he turned to his trusty Magic 8-Ball. "Should I schedule the meeting for Monday?" – "Better not tell you now." So, he didn't. The accidental result? His team resolved their issues independently, boosting their problem-solving skills. Lesson learned: A Magic 8-Ball might just be the unsung hero of management.

Case Study 3: The Director Who Flipped a Coin for a Marketing Strategy

Director Sarah, torn between two marketing strategies, decided to flip a coin. Heads for Strategy A, tails for B. It landed on heads, and Strategy A it was. The campaign was moderately successful – not groundbreaking, but not a flop either. Lesson learned: Sometimes, leaving it to chance leads to pleasantly average results.

Case Study 4: The Executive Who Based a Product Launch Date on Her Horoscope

Diana, an executive, had to choose a product launch date. On a whim, she consulted her horoscope, which read, "Today's a 5-star day for new beginnings!" The launch was a hit, more due to market readiness than celestial alignment, but hey, stars don't lie.

Lesson learned: The cosmos might be a more reliable advisor than we give it credit for.

Each of these case studies highlights the unexpected charm and sometimes surprising effectiveness of mediocre decision-making. While not every lukewarm decision leads to success, these examples show that there's a certain beauty in embracing the art of the average, and often, a good laugh in the outcome.

The Power of Lowered Expectations

As we wrap up our foray into the world of mediocre decision-making, let's ponder the power of lowered expectations. In the high-pressure cooker of leadership, dialing down the expectation thermostat can lead to a more relaxed, and paradoxically, more effective leadership style. It's about embracing the Zen of 'good enough' and discovering that sometimes, the middle road leads to unexpected scenic views.

Lowered expectations in decision-making are like a secret backdoor to stress-free leadership. It's giving yourself the permission to not be perfect, to accept that not every decision is a do-or-die moment. This approach isn't about aiming for failure; it's about setting realistic targets and finding comfort in the knowledge that 'okay' is, in fact, okay. It's like choosing to walk peacefully through a meadow instead of sprinting up a mountain – both paths lead somewhere, but one is certainly more breathless than the other. And here's the twist: when you expect less from your decisions, you might just be pleasantly surprised more often. With the weight of perfection lifted, decisions flow more freely, creativity blooms in the space left by anxiety, and teams respond to the lowered pressure with a sense of ease and possibility.

Here's a playful call to action for all the leaders out there: embrace your inner mediocrity. Give yourself the gift of 'good enough' decision-making. Let go of the reins a bit and watch as your team and your work benefit from this newfound freedom. Remember, in the garden of leadership, not every flower needs to be a prize-winning rose; sometimes, a field of wildflowers, in all their imperfect glory, is just as breathtaking.

In conclusion, let's raise a glass to the art of 'good enough' decision-making. Here's to the leaders who find strength in flexibility, wisdom in simplicity, and success in the wonderfully average. May your decisions be as pleasantly mediocre as a well-worn pair of slippers – comfortable, reliable, and just right.

Chapter 7: Perfection: The Fast Track to a Nervous Breakdown

Introduction to the Perfection Paradox

Welcome to the paradoxical world of perfection in leadership – a land where the quest for flawless execution often leads to a carnival of chaos. This chapter opens the curtains on the great performance of perfection, revealing it as less of a heroic epic and more of a comedic opera.

Picture the pursuit of perfection as a treadmill that's always just a little too fast. Leaders hop on with dreams of impeccable outcomes, only to find themselves sprinting towards an unreachable finish line. It's a race where the prize is a mirage, and the only guarantee is a good pant.

The Tech Executive and the Never-Launched App:

There's a story from the tech world where an executive, let's call him David, was obsessed with launching the perfect app. He demanded countless revisions, insisted on the latest features, and was fixated on outdoing competitors. The development cycle became an endless loop of tweaks and changes. The punchline? By the time the app was "perfect," the market had moved on, and the app's once-innovative features were now standard. The app was a masterpiece of technological prowess, but it debuted in a world that had already left its cutting-edge ideas behind.

The Retail Manager and the Immaculate Store Display:

In the retail industry, there was a manager named Emily, known for her immaculate store layouts. Her attention to detail was legendary – every item was aligned, every display meticulously arranged. The store looked like a page from a catalog. However, her quest for perfection made rearranging or updating the store a painstakingly slow process. It became a running joke among staff that changing a window display took longer than the seasons outside. Customers appreciated the aesthetics but often found the store lagging in showcasing the latest trends.

These examples, while not tied to specific real-life individuals, demonstrate the pitfalls of perfectionism in leadership. They highlight the humor in the all-too-common scenarios where the pursuit of perfection leads to outcomes that are ironically counterproductive. These tales serve as cautionary reminders that the pursuit of perfection is often a recipe for complication. It's like baking a soufflé in an earthquake – ambitious, but probably ill-advised.

In leadership, perfection is a mirage in the desert of reality. It looks appealing from a distance, but get closer, and you'll find its just hot air. This chapter invites you to laugh at the absurdity of perfection, to embrace the beauty of flaws, and to remember that sometimes, the most perfect thing you can do is to accept that nothing really is perfect.

The Perfectionist Leader's Typical Day

Imagine a day in the life of a perfectionist leader, where every tick of the clock is an opportunity for over-analysis and every minor detail is a crisis waiting to happen. Let's take a comical, exaggerated stroll through their typical day:

6:00 AM: The alarm rings, tuned to the perfect decibel. Our leader wakes up and aligns their slippers at a flawless 45-degree angle to the bed.

6:15 AM: Breakfast is an exercise in precision: precisely 28 blueberries (no more, no less) and a slice of toast browned to the exact shade of Pantone 7504 C.

8:00 AM: Arriving at work, they spend 15 minutes aligning their parking spot, ensuring the car is centered down to the millimeter. 9:00 AM: In their first meeting, a presentation slide is a micrometer off-center. Chaos ensues. The meeting is derailed as our leader recalibrates the projector, turning a quick sync into a saga.

11:00 AM: Email time. Each response is crafted like a literary masterpiece, undergoing four rounds of edits before being deemed worthy of sending.

1:00 PM: Lunch is skipped – there's no time for food when the line spacing in a report isn't consistent.

3:00 PM: A team member suggests a small process change. What follows is a three-hour meeting, complete with flowcharts and a risk analysis, to evaluate this monumental proposal.

6:00 PM: Time to review the day's work. Every task is scrutinized, every decision dissected. The leader finds a typo in an internal memo and launches an investigation to prevent such a catastrophic oversight in the future.

9:00 PM: Bedtime, but sleep is elusive. The leader's mind races with thoughts of aligning paper clips in perfect parallel for tomorrow's big meeting.

This day is a whirlwind of micromanagement and an obsession with details that would make even a microscope feel inadequate. Our perfectionist leader, in their quest for flawlessness, turns molehills into mountains and PowerPoint slides into puzzles of precision.

The moral of the story? In the relentless pursuit of perfection, life becomes a comedy of errors, a constant chase after an unattainable ideal. Sometimes, it's okay to have 27 blueberries instead of 28, and a slightly off-center parking job won't cause the universe to implode. In the end, embracing a bit of imperfection might just be the key to a happier, healthier, and decidedly less eccentric leadership style.

Perfection in Decision-Making: Analysis Paralysis

In the realm of leadership, one of the most comical, yet frustrating, phenomena is 'analysis paralysis' – the art of overthinking decisions to the point where nothing gets decided. It's like standing in the cereal aisle at the grocery store for hours, agonizing over cornflakes versus granola. Now, let's explore this concept with a humorous twist, diving into fictional case studies of leaders caught in the whirlpool of decision-making perfectionism.

Case Study 1: The Great Coffee Conundrum

Meet CEO Margaret. Faced with the seemingly simple task of choosing a new office coffee brand, Margaret turned it into an epic saga. She organized taste tests, analyzed bean origins, and even delved into the environmental impact of coffee production. Employees joked that by the time Margaret made her decision, they'd all have retired or switched to tea. Two years later, Margaret triumphantly announced her choice – only to find out the company had moved on to a new trend: artisanal tea.

Case Study 2: The Email Signature Saga

Then there's the story of Jacob, a department head, who decided to revamp the company's email signature template. What started as a minor tweak turned into a year-long project. Jacob obsessed over font choices, the precise shade of the company logo, and the optimal number of social media icons. Meetings were held, surveys were sent, consultants were called in. When the new signature was finally rolled out, it was met with a resounding response of, "It looks the same as the old one."

Case Study 3: The Never-Ending Office Layout Debate

Finally, we have Sarah, a manager tasked with redesigning the office layout. Determined to create the perfect workspace, Sarah's pursuit of perfection led to endless floor plan revisions, 3D models, and even a virtual reality simulation of the office. Staff started taking bets on whether the new layout would be finalized before or after the lease on the building expired. In the end, the layout remained unchanged, but Sarah did win an unofficial award for the most detailed virtual office tour.

These exaggerated case studies highlight the absurdity of analysis paralysis in the quest for perfection. They serve as a humorous reminder that sometimes, the pursuit of the flawless decision is like trying to catch a unicorn – enchanting to think about, but ultimately, a wild chase leading nowhere.

While meticulous decision-making has its place, there's a fine line between being thorough and falling into the comical trap of analysis paralysis. Sometimes, the best decision is the one that's made – even if it's just picking a coffee brand or an email signature.

The Quest for the Perfect Team

In the fantastical world of leadership lore, there exists the fabled quest for the perfect team – a journey fraught with outlandish expectations and a hiring strategy that makes the Labors of Hercules look like child's play. Let's dive into the humorous misadventures that unfold when a leader sets impossibly high standards for team assembly.

Imagine a leader, let's call him Bob, who embarked on a quest to build the ultimate dream team. His criteria? Only the best of the best – think Nobel Prize laureates for entry-level positions, Olympic athletes for team coordinators, and chess grandmasters to handle the weekly schedule.

Bob's job postings read like a wish list for a fantasy sports team. For a basic data analyst role, the requirements included deciphering ancient hieroglyphics and mastery of at least seven languages – fictional ones included. The interview process involved a labyrinthine obstacle course (designed by a former game show host) and a roundtable discussion on solving world hunger – all before the first coffee break.

The result of such ludicrous standards was a revolving door of hiring and firing. Candidates who could actually meet the criteria were as rare as a unicorn in a city park. The few who did make the cut soon found themselves burnt out by Bob's relentless pursuit of team perfection, leading to a never-ending cycle of recruitment and farewell parties.

Bob's office became a legendary tale in the corporate world. Prospective candidates would hear about the 'Bob Gauntlet' and flee in the opposite direction. Meanwhile, Bob stood baffled, wondering why he couldn't retain his staff, unaware that his quest for the perfect team was more akin to chasing a mirage in a desert of unrealistic expectations.

The moral of this slightly exaggerated tale? In the quest for the perfect team, setting the bar impossibly high can lead to a comedy of errors. It's a reminder that while ambition is commendable, seeking perfection in team building is like trying to knit a sweater with spaghetti – ambitious, but ultimately futile. The best teams are built not on superhuman achievements, but on a blend of diverse talents, realistic expectations, and perhaps most importantly, a good sense of humor.

The Illusion of Perfect Leadership

In the annals of leadership, the myth of perfection looms large, casting an imposing shadow over mere mortals striving to lead effectively. It's time to puncture this balloon of illusion with a dose of humor and a reality check. Let's embark on a tongue-in-cheek critique of the elusive perfect leadership, featuring mock testimonials from some of history's greatest figures and beloved fictional superheroes.

Mock Testimonial 1: Julius Caesar

"Veni, vidi, vici? More like Veni, vidi, I forgot to update my to-do list. Conquering Gaul was easier than managing my Roman Senate calendar invites."

Mock Testimonial 2: Cleopatra
"Queen of the Nile, sure, but don't even ask about the state of my email inbox. Let's just say there's a reason I preferred communicating via rolled-up papyrus."

Mock Testimonial 3: Superman

"Faster than a speeding bullet, more powerful than a locomotive, but still can't find a way to balance my hero duties with my day job at the Daily Planet. X-ray vision doesn't help with time management, unfortunately."

Mock Testimonial 4: Elizabeth I

"They called me the Virgin Queen, but really, I was just too busy ruling an empire to update my relationship status. Perfect leadership? Hardly. I couldn't even perfect my court's dance routines."

As these testimonials reveal, even the most illustrious leaders and superheroes had their share of leadership hiccups. Perfection in leadership is as real as a unicorn galloping through Times Square.

Now, for a bit of fun, let's delve into the "Perfectionist Leader's Reality Check" quiz:

When making decisions, do you:
A) Consult the stars, your tarot cards, and your magic 8-ball?
B) Ask your team, then ask them again, just to be sure?
C) Decide on a whim – eeny, meeny, miny, moe style?

Your approach to delegation is:
A) What's delegation? If you want something done right, do it yourself.
B) Hand tasks off, then hover like a helicopter parent.

C) Delegate? Sure. That's why we have interns, right?

When faced with a challenge, you:
A) Panic internally while maintaining a stoic exterior.
B) Dive into a 500-page motivational self-help book.
C) Challenges? That's future me's problem.

If you answered mostly A's or B's, relax – perfection is overrated. If you chose C's, congratulations on embracing your perfectly imperfect leadership style. Remember, the best leaders aren't flawless; they're real, relatable, and occasionally, as chaotic as a cat herder.

Delegating for Perfectionists: Mission Impossible

In the paradoxical universe of perfectionist leaders, delegating tasks is akin to a mission impossible. It's a comedic ballet of control, micromanagement, and the inevitable surrender to doing it all themselves. Let's dive into the hilariously impossible world of delegation, as seen through the eyes of a perfectionist.

Picture a leader, let's call her Alice, who decides to delegate the simple task of ordering office supplies. However, Alice's instructions resemble more of a novel than a memo. The manual includes preferred pen brands (down to the ink viscosity), paper thickness specifications, and even the optimal stapler weight. Her team, bewildered by the labyrinthine instructions, collectively decides it's safer to let Alice handle it.

Then there's the story of Carl, a manager who needed a presentation done. He delegated it to his team, but not without a 20-page guideline on font choices, slide transitions, and the acceptable shade of blue for the graphs (sky blue, but not too sky-ish). The team attempted it, but after the 10th revision (and a debate over whether the blue was too 'oceanic'), Carl, in a fit of frustration, pulled an all-nighter to do it himself, muttering about the impossibility of finding good help.

And who can forget the tale of Deborah, the perfectionist project leader? She assigned a team member to draft a report, then proceeded to 'help' by rewriting the whole thing. The final product was impeccably perfect, every comma and period in its divine place. The original drafter's contribution? A distant memory, like a fleeting shadow in Deborah's quest for perfection. These comical scenarios highlight the Sisyphean struggle of perfectionist leaders in the realm of delegation. For them, letting go is like sending their child off to college – necessary, but fraught with worry and a barrage of 'just checking in' calls.

In the end, these leaders often find themselves trapped in a cycle of over-instruction and inevitable disappointment, only to take on the tasks themselves. The irony, of course, is that their pursuit of perfection in delegation often leads to the very imperfection they were trying to avoid – burnout, team frustration, and a never-ending to-do list that only they can tackle.

The Burnout Boulevard: Signs You're on It

As a leader with a penchant for perfection, it's easy to find yourself cruising down Burnout Boulevard, a road paved with obsessive attention to detail and towering expectations. Let's explore the telltale, albeit exaggerated, signs that you're speeding towards burnout, and introduce a mock 'Burnout Prevention Kit' for the perfectionist in every leader.

Sign 1: Desk Symmetry Obsession
You know you're on Burnout Boulevard when you spend more time aligning your desk items into geometric perfection than you do on actual work. If your desk isn't a mirror image from left to right, does the day even count?

Sign 2: The Color-Coding Conundrum
If every file, folder, and paperclip isn't color-coded according to a system so complex it requires its own manual, then brace yourself – you're en route to Burnout Town. Bonus points if you've ever color-coordinated your lunch to match your filing system.

Sign 3: Email Inbox Zero Zealot
Achieving Inbox Zero is your daily Everest. You treat each email like a foe to be vanquished. If an unread email dares linger past noon, it's a sign of impending chaos.

Sign 4: The Perfectionist's Calendar
Every minute of your day is scheduled, including time slots to think about scheduling. Spontaneity is your arch-nemesis; if it's not in the calendar, it doesn't exist.

To combat these burnout harbingers, we present the 'Burnout Prevention Kit':

Item 1: The Perfect Cube Stress Ball
Squeeze away your stress with a stress ball that's a perfect cube – because even your stress relief tools need to meet your high standards.

Item 2: The 'Let It Go' Singing Timer
This timer randomly belts out the chorus of 'Let It Go' to remind you to step back, breathe, and embrace a little imperfection now and then.

Item 3: The Emergency Glitter Bottle
When things get too intense, unleash a glitter bomb in your office. It's impossible to worry about perfection when you're finding glitter in your hair for weeks.

Item 4 : The 'Not Today' Rubber Stamp
Stamp this on overly ambitious to-do lists to remind yourself that it's okay to not do it all in one day. Tomorrow is another day, after all.

The journey down Burnout Boulevard is a common one for perfectionist leaders, but with a dash of humor and a pinch of perspective, it's possible to take a detour towards a healthier, more balanced leadership style.

Embracing Imperfection: A Sane Alternative

As our journey through the meticulously manicured gardens of perfectionism comes to an end, it's time to meander into the charmingly unkempt wilderness of imperfection. Embracing imperfection in leadership is not about lowering the bar, but rather about finding joy and creativity in the unpredictable dance of leadership.

The benefits of this approach are like hidden treasures in a sea of sameness. When you let go of the need for flawless execution, a surprising burst of creativity emerges. It's as if your mind, no longer constrained by the shackles of perfection, is free to explore, innovate, and take risks. This liberation isn't just good for you; it's a breath of fresh air for your team as well. They see a leader who is human, approachable, and understanding – a leader who values progress over perfection. This human touch can transform the atmosphere of a workplace, injecting a sense of camaraderie and shared purpose.

And let's not forget the personal peace that comes with this approach. Letting go of perfection is like turning off a non-stop, nagging inner voice. It's giving yourself permission to be human, to make mistakes, and to learn from them. This mindset fosters a healthier work-life balance, reduces stress, and makes leadership a more enjoyable and sustainable endeavor.

To help you embark on this journey, consider adopting a few practices that champion imperfection. Start your day with a reminder that 'good enough is great' – a mantra that serves as a shield against the onslaught of perfectionism. Wear mismatched socks as a playful symbol of your commitment to embracing life's little imperfections. Allow yourself only a handful of minutes on tasks that don't demand perfection – a practice that encourages decisiveness and efficiency.

Embrace the Oops moments. Every small mistake is an opportunity for growth, a chance to inject a bit of humor into your day. Set aside a regular time each week to reflect on what didn't go as planned and then consciously let it go. It's like a ritual cleansing of your perfectionist tendencies.

Stepping into the world of imperfect leadership is a journey worth embarking on. It's about celebrating the quirks, embracing the missteps, and finding the extraordinary in the ordinary. So, loosen up those tight reins of perfection, enjoy the ride, and watch as you and your team thrive in an environment where being perfectly imperfect is not just accepted, but celebrated.

Chapter 8: Embracing the Chaos: A Leader's Guide to Controlled Panic

Introduction to the World of Leadership Chaos

Welcome to the rollercoaster world of leadership, where the only constant is chaos and the ability to panic gracefully is a valued skill. Forget the serene images of leaders calmly navigating the ship; real leadership is more like juggling flaming torches while riding a unicycle on a tightrope. Let's embark on a whimsical journey through the unpredictable, often absurd world of leadership chaos.

Imagine a CEO, let's call her Barbara, starting her day with a meticulously planned schedule. By 9:05 AM, the schedule is a distant memory, lost in a sea of unexpected crises, urgent emails, and a mysteriously malfunctioning coffee machine. It's like planning a picnic and ending up in a food fight.

Then there's the story of a project manager, Alex, who thought managing a team would be like conducting an orchestra. Little did he know, it was more akin to herding cats while the cats are simultaneously learning to play the violin. Every day brings a new surprise – from missed deadlines to technology that seems to have a mind of its own.

And who can forget the legend of the marketing director, Nena, whose well-planned product launch turned into an impromptu comedy show when the keynote speaker accidentally activated the voice-altering filter. It was less of a product launch and more of an accidental venture into stand-up comedy.

These light-hearted anecdotes serve as a reminder that leadership isn't about creating a world free from chaos; it's about learning to dance in the storm, sometimes with your shoes on the wrong feet. It's a world where controlled panic isn't just a reaction, it's a strategy.

Buckle up and embrace the chaos. Leadership is less about mastering the art of order and more about becoming an aficionado of managing the unpredictable, all while maintaining a sense of humour and a semblance of sanity.

The Anatomy of a Leadership Crisis

In the unpredictable theater of leadership, crises follow a dramatic and often comical script. Let's dissect the typical stages of a leadership crisis, a journey from the calm "This is fine" to the chaotic "Everything is on fire." It's a narrative arc filled with twists, turns, and the occasional facepalm moment.

Stage 1: The Blissful Ignorance
It begins on a seemingly ordinary day. Our leader, let's call him Dave, sips his coffee, blissfully unaware of the storm brewing. It's the calm before the storm, where the biggest worry is whether to go for a second cup of coffee or not.

Stage 2: The Small Ripple
Suddenly, a minor issue pops up. Perhaps it's an email about a missed deadline or a small client complaint. Dave chuckles and mutters, "This is fine. A walk in the park." Little does he know, it's more like a walk in a park that's about to host a rock concert.

Stage 3: The Snowball Effect
The minor issue quickly snowballs. The missed deadline was for a major project, and the client complaint has gone viral on social media. Dave's chuckle morphs into nervous laughter. "Still manageable," he insists, as he starts to feel like a chef trying to cook a five-course meal with only a toaster.

Stage 4: The Full-Blown Crisis

Now, we're in the thick of the crisis. Emails are flying, phones are ringing off the hook, and Dave's starting to resemble a cartoon character running on a treadmill – lots of movement but going nowhere fast. "Everything is under control," he says, in a voice that betrays his panic.

Stage 5: The Absurd Climax
In an almost comical twist, more problems pile on. The WiFi crashes, there's a typo in a public statement, and to top it off, someone accidentally sets off the fire alarm. It's less of a crisis now and more of a circus act gone rogue. Dave is now juggling flaming torches while riding that unicycle.

Stage 6: The Phoenix Rising
Finally, amidst the chaos, a solution emerges. It's not pretty – more duct tape and superglue than elegant craftsmanship – but it works. The crisis is averted, barely. Dave, battle-scarred but triumphant, emerges from the chaos, a little wiser and with a few more gray hairs.

The anatomy of a leadership crisis is a wild ride from tranquility to pandemonium. It showcases the unpredictable nature of leadership, where small issues can escalate into absurd crises. Leaders like Dave learn that managing a crisis often involves a sense of humor, a dash of creativity, and the resilience to ride through the storm – all while trying to avoid getting hit by lightning.

Creating Your Panic Schedule

In the tumultuous world of leadership, where crises lurk around every corner, there's an unconventional tool every leader should have: the 'Panic Schedule.' It's a mock-serious, tongue-in-cheek guide to organizing your daily freak-outs with the same precision you'd apply to a board meeting. Let's explore how to craft this essential tool, ensuring your moments of panic are as structured and efficient as the rest of your day.

Morning Panic (8:00 AM - 9:00 AM):

Start your day with a healthy dose of panic. Over your morning coffee, ponder the vast array of things that could go wrong today. This is your time to overthink, worry about missed emails, and contemplate the existential dread of your to-do list. It's like a warm-up exercise, but for anxiety.

Mid-Morning Overreaction Hour (11:00 AM - 12:00 PM):
This slot is reserved for overreacting to minor issues. Did someone misspell a word in a report? Is the printer jammed again? Now's the time to treat these small inconveniences as catastrophic events. Remember, it's not an overreaction; it's an enthusiastic response to mundane problems.

Lunchtime Lament (1:00 PM - 2:00 PM):
Lunch break is the perfect time for a midday lament. Reflect on the morning's panic, ponder the meetings that went sideways, and worry about the decisions you've made. It's like a lunch buffet, but instead of food, you're serving up a plate of worries and second-guessing.

Afternoon Anxiety (3:00 PM - 4:00 PM):
As the day progresses, allocate time for general anxiety. This is a flexible slot; feel free to worry about anything from upcoming deadlines to that awkward interaction by the water cooler. It's an open forum for all your concerns – the more, the merrier!

Evening Meltdown (6:00 PM - 7:00 PM):
Wind down your day with a scheduled meltdown. This is when you contemplate the existential crises of leadership. Ponder the big questions: Are you doing enough? What is the meaning of all this? It's a time for deep reflection and maybe a little bit of existential panic.

Bedtime Worry Wind-Down (10:00 PM - 11:00 PM):
Finally, as you prepare for bed, engage in a worry wind-down. Think about tomorrow and all the potential chaos it might bring. It's like counting sheep, but instead, you're counting potential problems.

Remember, a well-organized Panic Schedule is the key to controlled chaos. It's about embracing the madness of leadership with a sense of humor and a dash of self-awareness. So, plan your panic, schedule your stress, and remember to laugh in the face of leadership chaos – it's all part of the ride.

The Emergency Chocolate Break

In the high-stakes theater of leadership, amidst the drama of deadlines and the comedy of unexpected hiccups, there lies a secret weapon of sweet relief: the 'Emergency Chocolate Break.' This delightful strategy for immediate stress alleviation is more than just a whimsical indulgence; it's a tactical pause, a moment of cocoa-infused calm in the storm of leadership chaos. Let's delve into the art of choosing the right chocolate for each crisis and the wisdom of maintaining a covert stash for various emergencies.

Consider the mild panic situations – a misdirected email or a minor scheduling snafu. These call for the gentle comfort of milk chocolate, a soothing balm for the slight ruffles in your leadership journey. It's like a soft pat on the back, reassuring you that this too shall pass.

When the stress deepens, when you're steering through the tumultuous waters of a significant project setback or grappling with a challenging team dynamic, dark chocolate stands as your stalwart companion. Its rich, intense essence mirrors the depth of your stress, offering a moment of contemplative reprieve, a bittersweet armor against the trials of leadership.

For those whimsical worries, the light-hearted missteps that add a dash of humor to your day, white chocolate is your ally. Its creamy, sweet disposition is perfect for laughing off those minor blunders, a reminder not to take everything too seriously.

During crunch times, when the pressure mounts and deadlines loom, a chocolate bar with nuts is the perfect counterpart. The satisfying crunch echoes the intensity of the moment, a crunchy chorus to the symphony of your leadership challenges.

And for the fiery emergencies, those red-alert moments that test your mettle, chili chocolate is your secret weapon. The spice invigorates your senses, a fiery nod to your capability to handle even the most heated situations with grace. Above all, the discerning leader knows the value of a secret chocolate stash, an array of cocoa-based remedies for every level of crisis. Hidden in a desk drawer or behind a stack of reports, this stash is your emergency kit, a sweet arsenal against the unpredictabilities of leadership.

In embracing the 'Emergency Chocolate Break,' you acknowledge the importance of taking a step back, of savoring a moment of chocolate-induced serenity amidst the chaos. It's a strategy that goes beyond indulgence; it's about finding joy and resilience in the small things, about facing the whirlwind of leadership with a hint of sweetness and a renewed spirit.

The Art of Overreaction

In the grand theater of leadership, the art of overreaction is like an unexpected plot twist – sometimes, making a mountain out of a molehill is not just entertaining, but strategically sound. Let's dive into the whimsical world of leadership overreaction, where blowing things out of proportion is not a flaw, but a flair. Here, we offer playful advice on mastering this art, along with humorous scenarios where an over-the-top reaction could, ironically, save the day.

Imagine a scenario where the office printer jams – a common nuisance. But in the hands of an overreaction maestro, this becomes an opportunity for a heroic saga. Summon the team, declare a state of emergency, and lead a dramatic mission to rescue the office from the tyranny of the paper jam. It's not just fixing a printer; it's an epic battle against the forces of office anarchy. The result? A team united by a common (albeit exaggerated) enemy, and a mundane problem transformed into a tale of triumph.

Then there's the case of a missed minor deadline. While a simple rescheduling would suffice, why not seize the chance for a

Shakespearean display of leadership? Call an urgent meeting, lament the fleeting nature of time, and passionately rally your troops to redeem this momentary lapse. It's a performance that would make Hamlet look tame, but it's also a distraction from the daily grind, a chance for the team to indulge in a bit of drama, and perhaps, a good laugh.

Or consider the moment when a team member brings in a new type of coffee for the office. Instead of a mere nod of approval, launch into a grandiose speech about innovation and the courage to break from tradition. It's not just a new coffee flavor; it's a symbol of the team's pioneering spirit, a caffeinated metaphor for daring to think outside the box.

In mastering the art of overreaction, the key is to embrace the absurdity. It's about taking a small issue and giving it the spotlight, not because it's a crisis, but because it's a chance to inject some humor and theatrics into the workplace. It's a reminder that leadership doesn't always have to be about stoicism and solemnity; sometimes, it can be about playfulness, creativity, and a touch of well-timed melodrama.

So, next time a minor issue arises, consider the art of overreaction. Inflate the problem, add a dash of drama, and watch as a mundane moment transforms into a memorable adventure. It's a strategy that says, "Yes, we take our work seriously, but we also know how to laugh, especially at ourselves."

The Illusion of Control: Holding the Reins of Chaos

In the high-speed chase of leadership, the illusion of control is like holding onto the reins of a wild horse, convinced you're guiding it, while in reality, you're just along for the ride. This delusion isn't just a common experience; it's practically a leadership rite of passage. With a dash of humor, let's explore this curious phenomenon where leaders often find themselves gripping the reins of chaos, only to realize they're part of a much wilder journey.

Picture a leader, let's call him Jack, striding into a meeting with the confidence of a cowboy in an old Western. He thinks he's got the plan, the team, and the project firmly in his grasp. But as the meeting unfolds, with questions flying and problems mounting, Jack realizes he's more rodeo clown than cowboy. The project, much like a bucking bronco, has a mind of its own, and Jack's carefully laid plans are about as useful as a screen door on a submarine.

Amidst this chaos, leaders like Jack often adopt some creative tactics to maintain a semblance of control. One classic move is the 'Confident Nod' – a technique where you nod sagely at complex charts and data, giving the impression of deep understanding, when in reality, you're thinking about what to have for lunch.

Then there's the art of deploying buzzwords. Phrases like 'synergy,' 'pivot,' and 'streamline' are thrown into conversations like magical incantations, hoping to dazzle and distract from the fact that the reins of control are slipping. It's a linguistic dance, a ballet of jargon that sounds impressive but often means little. And let's not forget the strategic use of the 'Thoughtful Pause' – a moment where the leader, faced with a challenging question, pauses and looks contemplatively into the distance. It's a moment to gather thoughts, yes, but also to buy time and perhaps quickly formulate an escape plan.

The key takeaway in embracing the illusion of control is to recognize the humor in the chaos. It's about understanding that leadership is less about having all the answers and more about riding the waves of unpredictability. It's a mix of preparation, adaptability, and the ability to laugh when, despite your best efforts, the horse decides to run in the opposite direction.

While the reins of chaos may be slippery and the ride unpredictable, the savvy leader knows that sometimes, the best thing to do is hold on, enjoy the ride, and maybe even learn a thing or two along the way. After all, leadership is not just about steering the ship; it's also about sailing the seas of uncertainty with a smile and a sense of adventure.

Mandatory Meltdown Meetings

In the whimsical world of leadership where stress can be as common as coffee breaks, a novel concept emerges: 'Mandatory Meltdown Meetings.' These are specially designated gatherings where team members are encouraged to collectively embrace their panic and stress in a controlled, albeit slightly absurd, environment. It's like a pressure release valve for the workplace, a sanctioned space for letting off steam with a touch of humor and solidarity.

Imagine walking into a meeting room, the agenda is clear: No solutions, no judgments, just pure, unadulterated meltdown. The meeting kicks off with the first agenda item: "Complain about everything." This is the moment where everyone gets to air their grievances, from the existential dread of unread emails to the mystery person who keeps leaving half-empty coffee cups in the meeting room. It's a chorus of complaints, a symphony of stress, where the only rule is to let it all out.

Next up, the "Group Hyperventilation Session." Picture this: a circle of professionals, each taking turns to dramatically overreact to their latest work challenges. It's a blend of theatrics and therapy, where hyperventilating over printer jams or missed deadlines is not only accepted but encouraged. It's a moment of shared absurdity, a chance to laugh at the small stuff.

Then, there's the "Worst-Case Scenario Brainstorm." In this part of the meeting, team members compete to come up with the most exaggerated, unlikely disasters that could befall their projects. It's like a storytelling session, but with a flair for the catastrophic. The winner is the one who can make the others laugh the hardest with their creative doom and gloom.

As the meeting draws to a close, there's a sense of camaraderie in the air. The team has laughed, complained, and overreacted together. It's a reminder that sometimes, the best way to deal with stress is to face it head-on, with a group of people who understand what you're going through.

'Mandatory Meltdown Meetings' offer a unique approach to handling workplace stress. They create a space where it's okay to not be okay, where the pressures of perfection can be momentarily forgotten, and where laughter becomes the best medicine. So, next time the stress levels are high, consider calling a Meltdown Meeting – it might just be the most productive unproductive meeting you ever have.

The Leader's Guide to Impromptu Problem Solving

In the high-stakes game of leadership, the ability to think on your feet is crucial, but who says it can't be fun? Enter the 'Leader's Guide to Impromptu Problem Solving,' a handbook filled with comical, yet surprisingly effective, strategies for those times when conventional methods just won't cut it. It's about embracing the absurd to find creative solutions, turning the boardroom into a game room.

Rock-Paper-Scissors Decision-Making:
Caught in a deadlock over which marketing strategy to choose? Forget lengthy discussions; bring on the rock-paper-scissors showdown. It's quick, it's democratic, and let's face it – there's something thrilling about solving corporate conundrums with a game you played in the schoolyard.

Magic 8-Ball Consultation:
For those moments of indecision, why not consult the oracle of the office – the Magic 8-Ball? Shake it up and ask your burning question. "Should we increase our ad budget?" "Reply hazy, try again." It's a way to inject a bit of mystery (and a few laughs) into the decision-making process.

Dartboard of Destiny:
When the path forward is unclear, let the Dartboard of Destiny decide. Pin your options on the board, grab a dart, and let fate take the lead. It's a method that adds an element of chance to your choices and is sure to get the team talking (and maybe even cheering).

The Wheel of Solutions:
Create a wheel with a variety of out-of-the-box solutions and spin it when faced with a particularly thorny problem. Options could range from "Delegate to the intern" to "Brainstorm session in complete silence" or "Solve it with interpretive dance." It's a playful way to break out of traditional thinking patterns.

The Idea Lottery:
Everyone submits their solution to a problem on a slip of paper, and you draw one (or more) at random. It's a lottery where the jackpot is a fresh, unexpected approach to your challenge. Plus, it gives everyone a chance to contribute, adding to the inclusive and fun atmosphere.

Blindfolded Brainstorming:
For a truly unorthodox approach, try blindfolded brainstorming. Without the distractions of the room, team members can speak freely and creatively. It's a trust exercise, a brainstorming session, and a memorable team-building activity all rolled into one.

While these impromptu problem-solving strategies are certainly unconventional and lighthearted, they serve a deeper purpose. They encourage thinking outside the box, foster team engagement, and remind leaders that sometimes, the most creative solutions come from the most unexpected places. So, next time you're in a bind, remember: a little humor and a dash of creativity can go a long way in solving even the toughest of problems.

Embracing Chaos as the New Normal

In the grand finale of our exploration into the whimsical world of leadership, it's time to take a bow and accept that chaos isn't just an occasional guest; it's the new normal. Embracing chaos in leadership is like accepting that your GPS will invariably lead you through some strange routes – it's baffling, unpredictable, and sometimes takes you through the scenic route when you're already late.

Let's face it, the leader's journey is less of a tranquil cruise and more of a rollercoaster ride in an amusement park run by mischievous pixies. It's a world where plans are more like suggestions, and the unexpected is just another Monday (or Tuesday, or any day, really). So, why not embrace this madness with open arms?

Imagine starting your day with a chuckle instead of a sigh, knowing that whatever happens, you're in for an adventure. Picture team meetings where, amidst the chaos of conflicting ideas and sudden crises, there's an underlying current of excitement and a shared sense of "We're all in this together."

As a leader, embracing chaos means being ready to pivot at a moment's notice, like a nimble dancer on the stage of unpredictability. It's about finding joy in the whirlwind, recognizing that sometimes the best ideas and solutions emerge in the midst of mayhem. It's leading not with a rigid plan, but with adaptability, resilience, and a healthy dose of humor.

Remember to laugh in the face of chaos, or at least smile. Embrace the unexpected plot twists, the sudden detours, and the occasional moments of "What on earth is happening?" After all, leadership isn't just about steering the ship through calm waters; it's also about sailing through storms, sometimes with a leaky boat, but always with a spirit of adventure and a smile on your face.

The true art of leadership lies in riding the waves of chaos, turning challenges into opportunities, and remembering that sometimes, the best response to the madness is a good, hearty laugh. Welcome to the new normal – it's chaotic, it's unpredictable, and it's surprisingly fun.

Chapter 9: The Leader's Guide to Faking It Until You Make It

Introduction to 'Faking It' in Leadership

Embark on a journey into the secret world of leadership, where 'faking it' isn't just a tactic; it's a crucial skill, artfully blended into the fabric of management. Here, we'll explore the humorous yet essential role of pretending in leadership, where projecting confidence often precedes actual expertise, and a well-played act can be as effective as years of experience.

Imagine the early days of a startup founder, let's call him Mike. In investor meetings, Mike exuded confidence, talking about growth projections and market domination with the poise of a seasoned CEO. Little did they know, his business plan was more guesswork than data, his projections more hopeful than calculated. Yet, it was his feigned confidence that won the day, securing the funding needed to transform his bluffs into business successes.

Or consider the story of a newly appointed manager, Sara. On her first day, she walked into the office with a stride that screamed authority. In reality, she was a bundle of nerves, her leadership experience limited to leading discussions in book clubs. But in the boardroom, she was all business, her uncertainty hidden behind a mask of assuredness. Her team, none the wiser, followed her lead, believing in the persona she projected.

Then there's the anecdote of a marketing director, Alec, who was tasked with leading a campaign in an industry he knew little about. In meetings, he nodded sagely at industry jargon, throwing in an occasional buzzword he picked up from a quick Google search. His secret? Confidence and a crash course in industry lingo the night before. Alec's 'fake it' approach wasn't about deception; it was about buying time to turn his facade into expertise.

These stories highlight a less-talked-about aspect of leadership – the art of 'faking it' as a steppingstone to 'making it.' In the following chapters, we'll dive into how leaders can use this strategy effectively, balancing the act of projecting confidence with the journey of gaining real competence. It's about understanding that sometimes, in leadership, the best way to become confident is to first act confident.

The Art of Confident Confusion

In the intricate dance of leadership, there's a subtle but powerful move known as the 'Art of Confident Confusion.' It's the skill of not quite knowing what's going on but cloaking that confusion in a veil of confidence. This chapter is a lighthearted guide on mastering this art, blending ignorance with assurance in a way that can only be described as leadership ballet.

Picture yourself in a high-stakes meeting. A question flies at you, one you don't have the answer to. Instead of panicking, you lean into your confident confusion. You sit back, arms confidently crossed, with a thoughtful look that says, "I'm pondering your question," while your brain scrambles for an answer. It's the posture of certainty, the embodiment of the phrase, "Fake it till you make it."

Then there's the art of strategic mumbling. When asked for your opinion on a subject you know little about, respond with a mumble that sounds vaguely like industry jargon. "Well, the market dynamics are... quite complex," you murmur, nodding sagely. It's not about misleading; it's about buying time as you swiftly navigate the seas of your own uncertainty.

Another key element is the strategic use of buzzwords. When in doubt, throw in terms like "synergy," "pivot," and "streamline." These words are like the smoke and mirrors of leadership – they sound impressive and give you a moment to collect your thoughts. It's like a magician's flourish, diverting attention while you pull the rabbit out of the hat.

And let's not forget the power of redirecting the conversation. When faced with a challenging question, pivot gracefully to a related topic you're more comfortable with. It's a deft maneuver, turning a potential moment of exposure into an opportunity to steer the dialogue in a direction you can control.

Mastering the Art of Confident Confusion is about walking the tightrope between ignorance and confidence. It's a survival skill in the leadership jungle, a way to maintain your composure and authority, even when internally, you're navigating through a fog of uncertainty.

In the end, this art is not about deception; it's about maintaining your leadership presence and buying yourself time to find the answers. It's about embracing the fact that you won't always have all the answers – and that's perfectly okay. So next time you find yourself in the deep waters of confusion, remember: a confident exterior can be your life raft.

Mastering the Vague Response

In the intricate dance of leadership, one of the most elegant steps is mastering the art of the vague yet confident response. It's the ability to navigate tough questions with answers that are as enigmatic as they are assured. This chapter will guide you through the nuances of crafting responses that are both non-committal and impressively assertive, a verbal sleight of hand that leaves your audience both baffled and bedazzled.

Imagine you're in a meeting or interview, and a curveball question comes your way. Instead of stumbling for specifics, you lean into the power of ambiguity. Start with a classic like, "That's a great question, and we're exploring a variety of avenues to address it." It's a response that says, "I'm on top of it," even when your mind is sifting through possible answers like a frantic librarian in a vast, disorganized library.

Or, when pressed for details on a project's progress, respond with a confident, "We're pushing the envelope on that front and seeing some interesting developments." It's as vague as it is intriguing, a verbal smokescreen that hints at progress without getting bogged down in the mundane details.

Here are a few ambiguous yet impressive-sounding phrases to add to your leadership lexicon:

- "We're strategically positioning ourselves in a dynamic landscape."

- "It's about synergizing our core competencies to leverage potential outcomes."

- "Our approach is to proactively engage with emerging trends and pivot as necessary."

- "We're committed to cultivating a holistic understanding of the challenge."

- "It's essential to align our objectives with the fluidity of the market."

These phrases are like the Swiss Army knife of responses – versatile, multi-purpose, and always handy in a tight spot. They give the impression of insight and control, even when the specifics are as clear as mud.

Mastering the Vague Response is an art form that requires practice, poise, and a touch of creativity. It's about walking the fine line between saying something and saying nothing at all, all while maintaining an air of authority and confidence. It's a skill that can turn the most daunting of questions into an opportunity to display your leadership finesse.

So, the next time you're faced with a tough question, remember: vagueness, wielded with confidence, can be your secret weapon. It's not about misleading; it's about maintaining your composure and keeping your cards close to your chest, all while giving the illusion of transparency and control.

The Illusion of Informed Decision-Making

One of the most crucial acts is creating the illusion of informed decision-making. It's a performance where appearing knowledgeable is just as important as being knowledgeable. This chapter will take you through the art of skillfully deflecting or redirecting questions you can't answer and will provide a humorous look at how leaders sometimes make decisions based on the thinnest slivers of understanding.

Imagine you're in a high-stakes meeting, and you're asked about a topic you're less familiar with. Instead of admitting your lack of knowledge, you employ the strategic deflection. "That's an important point," you might say, "and it ties into a broader strategy we're developing. Let's circle back to that after we've discussed the overall direction." It's a deft move that buys you time and shifts the focus away from your momentary ignorance.

Or consider the tactic of redirecting. When pressed for details on a specific issue, you might respond, "That's just one piece of the puzzle. Let's look at how this fits into the bigger picture." It's a way of steering the conversation into familiar waters, where you can navigate more confidently.

Now, let's explore some humorous examples of leaders making decisions with only a superficial understanding of a situation. Picture a CEO who decides to rebrand the company based solely on a trending color scheme he saw on social media. "If it's good enough for Instagram, it's good enough for us," he declares, blissfully unaware of the nuances of branding.

Or the manager who decides to overhaul the IT system after overhearing a conversation about cloud computing at a coffee shop. Armed with buzzwords and a vague notion of 'the cloud,' she dives into a decision that leaves the IT department scratching their heads.

These examples highlight the often-comical reality of leadership, where decisions aren't always the product of deep analysis but are sometimes made on the fly, with just enough information to seem informed. It's a tightrope walk between appearing decisive and being recklessly impulsive.

The illusion of informed decision-making is a skill, a balancing act of appearing knowledgeable while quickly learning on the job. It's about projecting confidence, even when your knowledge is as thin as a sheet of paper. It's not about dishonesty; it's about maintaining your leadership image while you fill in the knowledge gaps.

The next time you face a question that leaves you stumped, remember: a confident deflection or a strategic redirect can be your best friends. In the end, leadership is as much about perception as it is about reality, and sometimes, creating the illusion of informed decision-making is an essential part of the show.

Building a Team to Compensate for Your Shortcomings

One of the most graceful moves is building a team that compensates for your own shortcomings. It's an admission, albeit a humorous one, that you can't possibly know everything. This chapter delves into the importance of surrounding yourself with people who excel in areas where you're merely faking expertise, complete with amusing anecdotes about leaders who turned their ignorance into an asset by hiring the right team.

Picture a CEO, let's call him John, known more for his charisma than his technical knowledge. He once sat through a meeting nodding sagely to terms like 'machine learning' and 'blockchain,' his understanding of which was as clear as a foggy night. Recognizing his limitations, John assembled a team of tech whizzes and data gurus. The result? A perfect blend where his vision and their expertise propelled the company into the tech stratosphere.

Then there's the story of Linda, a marketing director with a flair for creativity but a blind spot for analytics. To cover this gap, she hired a data analyst so proficient that he could find meaningful patterns in a bowl of alphabet soup. Linda would often joke in meetings, "I bring the ideas, and he brings the reality check." It was this combination of dream and data that transformed their campaigns from good to groundbreaking.

Or consider the case of a startup founder, Alex, whose knowledge of finance was limited to knowing that 'assets are good and liabilities are bad.' Realizing that a business needs a bit more financial acumen, he brought on board a finance expert who could navigate balance sheets and tax codes in his sleep. Alex's decision to hire for his weaknesses turned his financial naïveté into a non-issue, allowing him to focus on his strengths.

These stories highlight a crucial yet often overlooked truth in leadership: acknowledging your weaknesses is a strength. By building a team that complements your skill set, you create a well-rounded, dynamic group capable of tackling a wide range of challenges. It's like assembling a superhero team, where each member brings a unique power to the table.

The moral here is to embrace your shortcomings and surround yourself with people who fill those gaps. It's not about knowing everything; it's about knowing who knows what you don't. So, take a leaf out of John, Linda, and Alex's books: Hire smartly, lead wisely, and remember that sometimes, the best thing a leader can do is admit, "I have no idea, but I know someone who does."

The Power of Looking Busy

In the grand pageant of leadership, the art of looking busy is akin to a masterful stage performance. It's about projecting an air of ceaseless activity and critical importance, even if, in reality, you're just juggling a collection of tasks that look more urgent than they are. This chapter offers a tongue-in-cheek guide to mastering the appearance of being perpetually busy, with a sprinkle of humor and a dash of harmless deceit.

The Prop Play: Folders of Importance

One classic strategy is the Prop Play. Carry around a folder or binder, stuffed not with confidential documents, but with blank or irrelevant papers. It's a simple yet effective prop that screams, "I'm carrying the weight of important decisions." Bonus points if you occasionally open it, furrow your brow, and nod gravely, as if pondering the fate of the company.

The Phantom Phone Check

Another staple in the busy leader's toolkit is the Phantom Phone Check. Regularly glance at your phone with an expression of mild concern or intense focus. It doesn't matter if you're actually just scrolling through old emails or looking at pictures of puppies wearing hats. What matters is the perception it creates: "Look how in-demand I am."

The Busy Walk

Perfect the Busy Walk, a brisk, purposeful stride that you employ whenever moving through the office. It's a walk that says, "I'm off to solve major problems," even if you're just heading to the break room for a coffee refill. The key is a furrowed brow and a quick nod to anyone you pass – it's the international sign of "I'd chat, but I'm swamped."

The Art of the Meaningless Meeting

Occasionally, schedule a meeting with a vague yet important-sounding title like "Strategic Synergy Alignment." The agenda? Non-existent. The purpose? To reinforce your image as a leader deeply involved in high-level discussions. It's a meeting where the most strategic decision might be choosing between donuts or bagels.

The Clipboard of Significance

Arm yourself with a clipboard, and periodically jot down notes while nodding solemnly. It doesn't matter if you're actually writing your grocery list. To the casual observer, you're making decisions of grave consequence. The clipboard is the scepter of the busy leader, a symbol of authority and industriousness.

While these tactics are lighthearted and somewhat facetious, they highlight an underlying truth in corporate culture: the perception of busyness often equates to perceptions of effectiveness and importance. So, next time you feel the need to embody the essence of a busy leader, remember these playful strategies. It's about striking a balance between actual productivity and the art of looking the part.

Fake It Ethically: The Fine Line

Navigating the world of leadership often feels like walking a tightrope between confidence and candor. In this delicate balancing act, the concept of 'faking it' must be handled with care and integrity. This chapter delves into the ethical considerations of this strategy, underscoring the importance of truthfulness in your capabilities while maintaining a façade of confidence.

Consider yourself an ethical illusionist in leadership. Your act isn't about deceit; it's about performance, showcasing your strengths while being honest about what you don't know. This approach is akin to a magician who reveals the secret behind the trick, earning respect not just for the illusion but also for the honesty.

At the core of ethically 'faking it' lies the Honesty Clause: being truthful about your abilities. Admitting ignorance can often be more powerful than pretending knowledge. It's a strategy that builds trust and credibility, where saying "I don't know, but I'll find out" is more effective than making up answers. This transparency can paradoxically enhance your appearance of competence.

Maintaining a façade of confidence is essential, but it should be a thin veil, not a heavy mask. Let your confidence reflect your eagerness to learn and improve, rather than an attempt to cover up gaps in your knowledge. It's about projecting "I can handle this" rather than "I know everything about this," showcasing leadership grounded in realism rather than arrogance.

When you do need to project confidence, do so with finesse. It's a temporary tool to bridge gaps in expertise, not a permanent solution. This tactic is about buying time to develop the necessary skills, a stopgap rather than a standard practice.

Faking it ethically in leadership is about walking a fine line with grace and integrity. It's about balancing the act of appearing confident with the reality of continuous learning and growth. It's not about deceiving but about leading with a blend of humility, assurance, and above all, honesty. This fine line, though challenging, is the hallmark of a leader who values authenticity as much as efficacy.

Learning on the Fly: Turning Faking into Making

In the ever-evolving landscape of leadership, 'faking it' can often be the first step on the journey to 'making it.' This chapter is about embracing the act of faking as a springboard for learning, a kind of on-the-job training in disguise. It's about turning the façade of confidence and competence into the real deal, one challenge at a time.

Consider the story of Gladis, a young manager thrust into a role well above her experience level. Initially, her days were filled with confident nods and strategic silence. However, behind the scenes, Emily was on a steep learning curve, devouring books, seeking mentorship, and absorbing every piece of knowledge she could. Her façade of confidence was the armor she wore while building her skills in the shadows. In time, Emily transformed her act into actual expertise, her once-feigned confidence becoming a genuine reflection of her ability.

Then there's the tale of Bart, who landed a project management role by overstating his experience. In meetings, he was the epitome of calm and control, but privately, he was scrambling, learning project management tools and techniques late into the night. His journey from faking it to making it was a marathon of rapid learning and adaptation, fueled by the initial bluff that got him the job.

Or the anecdote of Fred, a marketing director who confidently pitched a digital strategy he barely understood. To avoid being exposed, Fred immersed himself in digital marketing courses, sought advice from experts, and gradually built a solid understanding of the field. His initial bluff became a self-fulfilling prophecy, turning him into the digital savant he initially pretended to be.

These stories highlight a key aspect of leadership: the initial act of 'faking it' is not a terminal destination but a starting point. It's a catalyst for growth, a push out of the comfort zone, and a challenge to expand your capabilities. Faking it, when coupled with a relentless pursuit of learning and improvement, can evolve into genuine expertise.

'Learning on the Fly' is about leveraging the act of faking as a tool for real development. It's about not letting the initial lack of knowledge or experience hinder your progress but using it as motivation to grow into the leader you aspire to be. So, as you navigate the act of faking, remember that each step, each pretended confidence, is an opportunity to learn, improve, and ultimately, make it for real.

Embracing the 'Fake It' Philosophy

As we draw the curtains on this exploration of the 'fake it till you make it' philosophy in leadership, it's time to take a step back and appreciate this approach not as a mere act of deception, but as a valuable steppingstone on the journey to genuine confidence and capability. This conclusion is a light-hearted endorsement of this strategy, coupled with a reminder of its true purpose in the grand theater of leadership.

The 'fake it till you make it' philosophy is akin to a fledgling actor taking on a challenging role. At first, the lines are recited with uncertainty, the character a mere sketch. But with each performance, the actor grows into the role, the lines become second nature, and the character comes to life. Similarly, in leadership, faking it is like rehearsing a part you aspire to perfectly play one day. It's a starting point, a push towards becoming the leader you envision.

Throughout this book, we've seen humorous examples and shared strategies on how to navigate the complexities of leadership by initially faking confidence or competence. However, the heart of this philosophy lies in its transformative power – the act of faking it is a catalyst for personal and professional growth. It's about using the guise of confidence to build real confidence, leveraging the act of pretending as a motivator to develop true capability.

While 'faking it' can be a useful tool in a leader's arsenal, it's crucial to remember that the ultimate goal is not to perpetually fake it, but to grow, learn, and evolve into the leader you're pretending to be. It's about embracing the journey from imitation to authenticity, from uncertainty to mastery.

As you step into the spotlight of leadership, equipped with the 'fake it till you make it' philosophy, remember that each step of pretense is an opportunity for real growth. It's a chance to stretch your limits, expand your horizons, and gradually transform into the confident, capable leader you aspire to be. Embrace the act, but never lose sight of the goal: genuine leadership excellence.

Chapter 10: The Joy of Lowered Expectations

Redefining Success: The Beauty of 'Good Enough'

Welcome to the final chapter, where we take a lighthearted dive into the concept of redefining success. In the high-stakes world of leadership, there's an unsung hero that often goes unnoticed: the beauty of 'good enough.' It's about embracing the joy of lowered expectations, a refreshing antidote to the relentless pursuit of perfection.

Picture a world where success isn't measured by overachieving or exceeding every goal, but by the simple satisfaction of doing 'good enough.' It's a world where the pressure is off, where you can breathe easy knowing that not every task needs to be a masterpiece. This chapter is an ode to the art of setting achievable goals and finding contentment in meeting them.

Let's take a whimsical look at leaders who have embraced this philosophy. There's the story of a manager, Sonia, who decided that her team meetings didn't need to be groundbreaking brainstorming sessions. Instead, they became brief check-ins, concise and to the point. The result? More time for actual work and less time spent in meetings that seemed to stretch into eternity.

Then there's the tale of a project leader, Max, who realized that his quest for the perfect presentation was causing undue stress. He opted for 'good enough,' which meant presentations that were clear and effective but didn't have the bells and whistles he once strived for. Surprisingly, his team responded better to this straightforward approach, appreciating the clarity and simplicity.

And let's not forget about Lisa, a CEO who decided to scale back her 12-hour workdays to a more manageable schedule. The fear was that productivity would plummet, but instead, she found that both she and her team became more efficient, as they were less burnt out and more focused.

Lowering expectations doesn't mean settling for mediocrity; it's about setting realistic goals and celebrating when you reach them. It's a shift from the exhausting chase for perfection to the satisfying embrace of the attainable. It's about finding joy in the journey, not just the destination.

The joy of lowered expectations is like a breath of fresh air in the often stifling atmosphere of leadership. It's a reminder that sometimes, 'good enough' is not just okay, but it's exactly what's needed. As we close this book, remember that redefining success isn't about lowering your standards, but about recognizing and savoring the beauty of the achievable, the realistic, and the wonderfully ordinary.

Redefining Success: The Beauty of 'Good Enough'

In a world obsessed with the mantra of 'more, better, faster,' let's take a whimsical pause to appreciate the underrated charm of 'good enough.' Redefining success isn't about lowering the bar; it's about realizing that sometimes the bar is set so unrealistically high that not even a pole-vaulting champion could clear it. This chapter is a light-hearted exploration of how embracing 'good enough' can lead to success that's not only more achievable but often more satisfying.

Imagine if success in leadership wasn't about outdoing yourself every quarter, but about meeting solid, realistic goals. It's like deciding to run a 5K race instead of aiming for a marathon when you've only ever jogged around the block. There's an unexpected joy in achieving these 'good enough' goals – a sense of satisfaction that comes from knowing you've done well, even if you haven't done everything.

Take the story of Mark, a team leader who always aimed for the stars but often ended up lost in space. He decided to try a different approach, setting more attainable targets for his team. To his surprise, not only did they hit these targets more consistently, but team morale soared. They celebrated these wins with pizza parties, where the toppings were as varied as the team's ideas – not extravagant, but perfectly satisfying.

Consider the case of Angela, a perfectionist CEO who believed that if a job wasn't done perfectly, it wasn't worth doing at all. One day, bogged down by her own expectations, she decided to try the 'good enough' approach. The result? Projects were completed on time, her evenings were no longer spent micromanaging, and she discovered the joys of hobbies forgotten since her youth, like gardening, where the flowers didn't always have to be in perfect rows to be beautiful.

These anecdotes show that lowering expectations doesn't mean compromising on quality; it's about reshaping our understanding of success. It's a shift from the unrelenting pressure of perfection to the liberating embrace of the attainable.

Let's carry with us the lesson of 'good enough.' It's a reminder to celebrate the small victories, to find contentment in what we've achieved, and to know that sometimes, good enough is not just good – it's great. Redefining success isn't about settling; it's about finding balance, joy, and a sense of achievement in a world that often asks for too much.

The Liberating Power of Lowered Expectations

In the relentless pursuit of excellence, there's an often-overlooked secret weapon: the liberating power of lowered expectations. This isn't about giving up on striving for greatness; it's about the freedom that comes from not needing everything to be perfect. In this part of the chapter, we dive into the humorous and freeing world where not aiming for the stars in every endeavor actually leads to less stress and, surprisingly, more enjoyment.

Consider the tale of Greg, a middle manager known for his meticulous attention to detail. Greg's motto was "If it's not perfect, it's not done," which translated to countless sleepless nights. One day, he decided to experiment with 'good enough.' The result? Reports were still thorough but completed on time, and Greg discovered the joys of evenings spent not poring over spreadsheets but playing guitar, an old hobby he'd neglected in his quest for perfection. His team noticed the change too – a happier, more relaxed boss, and a newfound appreciation for music (though Greg's singing still needed some work).

Then there's the story of Susan, a project coordinator whose events were legendary for their precision and extravagance. For her next event, she set a lower bar – less lavish, more manageable. To her amazement, the event was not only a success but also one of the most enjoyable she'd ever organized. Guests didn't miss the usual fanfare and actually welcomed the warmer, more relaxed atmosphere. Susan found herself actually mingling and laughing, rather than running around fixing last-minute details.

These scenarios highlight a simple truth: lowering expectations can be surprisingly liberating. It shifts the focus from the impossible task of making everything perfect to enjoying the process and accepting that good enough can be just that – good enough.

Embracing lowered expectations isn't about mediocrity; it's about discovering the joys of balance. It's a lesson in letting go of the unattainable ideal of perfection in every task and finding contentment in doing your best, without the crushing weight of having to be the best. So, as we wrap up this journey, let's remember that sometimes, the key to happiness and success in leadership, and life in general, lies in the power of lowered expectations – a power that can set us free.

Celebrating Mediocre Milestones

There's an often-underrated joy in celebrating the average, the mundane – the mediocre milestones. This part of the chapter is dedicated to injecting a bit of fun into the workplace by acknowledging and celebrating these unsung achievements in whimsical and humorous ways.

Imagine introducing a series of mock awards and ceremonies to honor the wonderfully ordinary feats of the office. Picture a monthly gathering where awards like the 'Most Adequate Report' are handed out with pomp and ceremony. The recipient, amid laughter and cheers, is awarded a golden stapler – not for outstanding work, but for work that was perfectly, gloriously adequate.

How about celebrating the 'Most Tolerable Meeting'? After a week of back-to-back meetings, the team votes for the one that was the least painful to sit through. The winning meeting organizer is crowned with a paper crown and given a scepter made out of highlighters, a light-hearted way to encourage efficient, bearable meetings.

Then there's the 'Okayest Idea of the Month' award, complete with a trophy that's intentionally a little crooked. It's given to the team member whose idea wasn't groundbreaking but contributed in a small, meaningful way. It's a celebration of the fact that not every idea needs to change the world; some just need to make the day a little bit better.

We could also introduce the 'Decent Effort' badge, given to someone who tried something new, even if it didn't quite work out as planned. It's a way of saying, "Hey, you gave it a shot, and that's worth something."

These whimsical celebrations serve a greater purpose than just laughs and light moments. They foster a culture where effort is appreciated, where it's okay to be average sometimes, and where the pressure to always excel is lifted, even if just for a moment. It's about creating an environment that values progress and effort over perfection, where every small step is recognized and celebrated.

Celebrating mediocre milestones is about finding joy in the little things, the everyday achievements that often go unnoticed. It's a reminder to teams that every contribution, no matter how small or average, is valuable. So, let's raise our slightly chipped mugs to the power of mediocrity, to the joy of being good enough, and to the shared laughter that comes from celebrating our most wonderfully ordinary accomplishments.

Lowering the Bar: A Step-by-Step Guide

In the final act of our journey through the wonders of mediocrity, let's roll out a satirical guide to lowering the bar. This is a tongue-in-cheek, step-by-step tutorial on how to set comfortably achievable goals and wholeheartedly embrace the 'meh.' It's about finding the sweet spot where lowered standards can paradoxically lead to higher team morale and increased productivity.

Step 1: The Great Goal Downsize
Start by revisiting your sky-high goals and asking, "Do we really need to climb Mount Everest, or is the local hill just fine?" Adjust these goals to more attainable levels. It's about distinguishing between what's nice to have and what's necessary.

Step 2: Celebrate the Small Wins
Learn to find joy in the small victories. Did everyone turn up to the meeting on time? Did the team manage to get through a whole day without the printer jamming? These are the wins worth celebrating. Break out the confetti for these modest yet morale-boosting achievements.

Step 3: The Power of 'Good Enough'
Embrace the power of 'good enough.' This doesn't mean producing subpar work; it's about recognizing when a task is completed to a satisfactory level and resisting the urge to over-polish. Remember, sometimes a homemade cake with lopsided icing is more charming than a store-bought masterpiece.

Step 4: Cultivating Comfortable Mediocrity

Encourage a culture where 'okay' is okay. It's a world where the phrase "That's good enough" is met with smiles, not frowns. It's about creating an atmosphere where the pressure to be perfect is replaced with the comfort of being good enough.

Step 5: The Joyful Release of Lowered Expectations
Experience the liberating feeling that comes with lowered expectations. Watch as team stress levels decrease and enjoyment in work increases. It's like removing a heavy backpack midway through a hike – suddenly, the journey becomes a lot more enjoyable.

Using irony and humor, this guide is not a call to embrace laziness or mediocrity, but an invitation to reevaluate and redefine what success looks like. It's about understanding that sometimes, by lowering the bar, we can actually jump higher. We create a work environment where people are free to do their best without the fear of not meeting impossibly high standards. Lowering the bar, when done right, can be a surprisingly effective strategy. It's about setting realistic expectations, celebrating the ordinary, and finding joy in the 'good enough.' So, as we bid farewell to the world of lowered expectations, remember, sometimes the best way to soar is to first adjust your wings.

The Art of Underwhelming Leadership

In corporate culture, there exists an unorthodox style that seldom makes headlines yet holds a certain charm: the art of underwhelming leadership. This approach, far from the high-octane, charisma-driven leadership often glorified, celebrates a more subdued, laid-back style. It's about understanding the unexpected benefits that come from dialing back the intensity and fostering a work environment that's relaxed, pressure-free, and surprisingly effective.

Underwhelming leadership isn't about being uninspiring or ineffective; rather, it's a strategy of leading with a quiet confidence that puts the team at ease. It's the leadership equivalent of a calming, steady hand in a world that often feels like a frantic, all-hands-on-deck situation.

One of the key benefits of this leadership style is the reduced pressure it places on team members. In an underwhelming leadership environment, employees don't feel the constant weight of overbearing expectations. Deadlines are important, but they're not doomsday clocks ticking down. Projects are necessary, but they're not relentless pursuits of perfection. This relaxed atmosphere often leads to increased creativity, as team members feel free to think outside the box without the fear of dramatic failure.

Underwhelming leaders are masters of setting a work pace that's steady but not frenetic. They appreciate the marathon more than the sprint, understanding that sustainable performance trumps short-term bursts of overexertion. They're like the tortoise in the age-old fable, who, despite its unassuming demeanor, wins the race.

The subtlety of underwhelming leadership also extends to recognition and rewards. Celebrations are sincere but not over-the-top. Achievements are acknowledged with a genuine pat on the back rather than a grand ceremony. It's a low-key approach that resonates with a sense of authenticity and down-to-earth appreciation.

The art of underwhelming leadership is about embracing a quieter form of influence. It's a nod to the power of subtlety in a world often captivated by the bold and the brash. As we wrap up this exploration of lowered expectations, remember that sometimes, the most effective leaders are those who don't aim to overwhelm but choose to wisely, and quietly, underwhelm.

The 'Good Enough' Leader's Manifesto

As we reach the end of our journey celebrating the 'good enough' leadership style, let's encapsulate this philosophy in a playful yet poignant manifesto. This is a declaration for all the leaders who have embraced their imperfections, who lead with a sense of humor, realism, and a refreshing dose of humility. Here's to the leaders who understand that sometimes, 'good enough' really is just right.

The 'Good Enough' Leader's Manifesto

1. I Pledge to Embrace the 'Meh' - I solemnly swear to recognize the beauty in the mediocre, the average, and the unremarkable. I will celebrate the small victories and find joy in the everyday achievements.

2. I Vow to Keep My Feet on the Ground - I promise to lead with a grounded approach, understanding that while my head may be in the clouds, my feet should always remain firmly planted on the earth of reality.

3. I Shall Lead with Laughter - I commit to maintaining a sense of humor in leadership, knowing that laughter can be a powerful tool in creating a positive and resilient team environment.

4. I Will Acknowledge My Imperfections - I accept that I am not infallible, and I will lead with an open acknowledgment of my flaws and a willingness to learn from them.

5. I Promise Not to Over-Promise - I vow to set realistic goals and expectations, both for myself and my team, steering clear of the pitfalls of over-promising and under-delivering.

6. I Will Celebrate 'Good Enough' - I pledge to appreciate the value of 'good enough,' understanding that perfection is a myth and that sometimes, doing a decent job is more than enough.

7. I Embrace the Art of Delegation - I commit to the art of strategic delegation, not as a sign of laziness, but as a recognition of my team's strengths and a way to empower them.

8. I Shall Foster a Relaxed Work Environment - I promise to cultivate a work culture where lowered expectations lead to increased creativity, productivity, and overall happiness.

In essence, the 'Good Enough' Leader's Manifesto is about leading with authenticity, humility, and a touch of light-heartedness. It's a commitment to leading not with an iron fist or a relentless pursuit of perfection, but with a warm smile and an understanding that in the grand scheme of things, good enough can lead to greatness.

Finding Joy in the Ordinary

In the final musings of our journey, let's turn our attention to one of the most understated yet essential aspects of 'good enough' leadership: finding joy in the ordinary. Amidst the endless pursuit of grand achievements and monumental successes, there lies a simple, often overlooked pleasure in the everyday tasks and small victories of leadership. This section is a gentle reminder, delivered with a lighthearted touch, to relish the simple, everyday moments that make up the tapestry of a leader's life.

Picture the quiet satisfaction in organizing a well-run, albeit unremarkable, meeting. There's no breakthrough innovation or standing ovation, but there's a sense of contentment in its smooth execution and the small nods of appreciation from your team. It's like enjoying a perfectly brewed cup of coffee on a quiet morning – nothing extraordinary, yet immensely satisfying.

Consider the small victories: the report submitted on time, the team conflict resolved with a simple conversation, the project that stayed on budget. These aren't headline-making achievements, but they're the bread and butter of effective leadership. They're like the quiet notes in a symphony – not the crescendos, but just as crucial to the overall harmony.

Remember to take pleasure in the simple aspects of your role. Enjoy the routine check-ins with your team, where you get to connect and share a laugh or two. Find delight in the everyday problem-solving, the regular rhythm of guiding your team through the ups and downs. It's like finding joy in a leisurely stroll, where the beauty lies not in the destination but in the journey itself.

Embracing the ordinary doesn't mean losing ambition or aspiration; it's about balancing the pursuit of excellence with an appreciation for the mundane. It's recognizing that leadership isn't just about the moments of triumph, but also about the quiet, consistent effort that underpins those successes.

Let's celebrate the unsung moments, the quiet accomplishments, and the simple pleasures of leading. For in these everyday experiences lies the true heart of leadership – not in the rare moments of glory, but in the daily, humble acts that keep the wheels turning and the team moving forward.

A Toast to Imperfection

As we bring the curtains down on this whimsical exploration of 'good enough' leadership, let's raise an imaginary glass in a toast to imperfection. Here's to the quirks, the idiosyncrasies, and the endearing flaws that make each leader uniquely themselves. It's a celebration of the unpolished, the unconventional, and the beautifully imperfect aspects of leading.

Picture us gathered in a grand hall, each with a glass in hand, ready to honor not the flawless execution of leadership, but the wonderfully human moments that define it. Imagine the clinking of glasses as we salute the missed deadlines that taught us time management, the awkward speeches that made us more relatable, and the failed projects that paved the way for future success.

"To the decisions made on the fly, to the projects that didn't quite hit the mark, and to the meetings that could have been emails," we cheer. "Here's to the leaders who aren't afraid to say, 'I don't know,' to those who lead more with heart than with a handbook, and to the ones who find strength in vulnerability."

This toast is an encouragement to embrace your own leadership style, no matter how unconventional it may be. It's a celebration of the fact that leadership isn't about being perfect; it's about being authentic. It's about recognizing that your unique approach, with all its quirks and eccentricities, is what makes you an effective leader.

Let's embrace our imperfections, not as hindrances, but as facets of our unique leadership identity. Let's lead with the knowledge that our flaws are not failings but features that add depth and character to our leadership style. In the end, remember, perfection is overrated, but authenticity never goes out of style. Here's to you, the 'good enough' leaders, the champions of the ordinary, the masters of the attainable, and the toast of the beautifully imperfect world of leadership.

Final Thoughts: Embracing the Journey

As we reach the end of this exploration into the world of 'good enough' leadership, it's time to reflect on the journey we've taken together. Leadership, as we've discovered, is not a quest for perfection but a journey of self-acceptance, growth, and embracing the unexpected detours and bumps along the way.

This book has been a celebration of the unpolished, the real, and the attainable in leadership. It's been a journey through the world of lowered expectations, where we've learned to find joy in the ordinary and to appreciate the beauty of being 'good enough.' We've laughed at the absurdity of perfection, raised a toast to our imperfections, and discovered the liberating power of embracing our authentic selves.

As you move forward in your leadership journey, remember the key messages we've shared. Embrace the quirks and flaws that make you unique. Celebrate the small victories and find humor in the challenges. Allow yourself to be 'good enough' and recognize that in doing so, you're more than just adequate – you're real, relatable, and effective.

Leadership is not about reaching a destination of flawlessness; it's about growing, learning, and finding fulfillment in the process. It's about leading with a sense of realism, understanding that the bumps along the way are not obstacles, but integral parts of the journey that shape us into the leaders we are meant to be.

This book is an invitation to enjoy your leadership journey, with all its imperfections and surprises. It's a call to step into the role of a 'good enough' leader – one who leads with authenticity, embraces growth over perfection, and finds joy in the everyday moments of leading.

We hope you carry forward the lessons learned, the laughter shared, and the acceptance of your beautifully imperfect journey. Remember, the path of leadership is not a straight line to perfection, but a winding road filled with learning, growth, and plenty of moments worth celebrating.

Continue Your Adventures in Leadership Land

Paradoxical Leadership

https://www.amazon.com/dp/B0CP3ZSPQS

Welcome to "Paradoxical Leadership," a groundbreaking exploration of leadership in its most unorthodox forms. This book is not your typical leadership manifesto. It delves deep into the heart of paradoxes, ironies, and unexpected truths that define leadership in the modern era. With a witty and engaging narrative, "Paradoxical Leadership" invites readers on a captivating journey through the multifaceted world of leadership, revealing the intricate tapestry of traits and decisions that shape effective leaders.

From genius tyrants to benevolent dictators, each chapter unveils real-life stories of leaders who defied conventional wisdom, showcasing the diverse ways in which leadership can manifest. Written with a blend of irony, wit, and profound insights, this book offers a fresh perspective on leadership, making it an enjoyable read for both seasoned executives and aspiring leaders. "Paradoxical Leadership" encourages readers to rethink traditional leadership narratives, emphasizing that effective leadership often resides in embracing contradictions and complexities. While exploring historical and contemporary leaders, the book distills practical lessons and insights, helping readers to apply these paradoxical principles in their own leadership journeys. Each chapter engages readers with vivid storytelling, challenging them to consider different aspects of leadership, from ethics and decision-making to innovation and personal growth.

Dive into "Paradoxical Leadership" and embark on a journey that transforms the way you think about leadership. Prepare to be enlightened, entertained, and inspired!

Note on Further Reading from Thomas Patrick Huber

Dear Reader,

If you've journeyed with me through the whimsical and unconventional exploration of leadership in this book and found yourself chuckling along the way, you might be wondering, "What's next?" For those of you who might be craving a more serious delve into the world of leadership, I have good news! Although, if you've enjoyed the entirety of this book, I have to wonder – just how serious can you be, right?

For a deeper dive into the realms of leadership, I invite you to explore my collection of more traditional leadership books. These works delve into various aspects of leadership with the seriousness and depth they deserve, providing insights and strategies for those looking to enhance their leadership skills and understanding.

You can find a comprehensive overview of my leadership books at the following homepage:

https://leadershipdevelopmentbooks.com

This collection is a treasure trove for anyone passionate about leadership, growth, and personal development. Whether you're looking to continue your leadership journey with a touch of humor or delve into more serious studies, there's a book waiting for you. Thank you for joining me on this delightful journey, and I hope to accompany you again in your next reading adventure.

Warm regards,

Thomas Patrick Huber, PhD MS ECS

About the Author

Dr. Thomas P. Huber, the healthcare management maestro and self-proclaimed leadership humorist, brings a dash of levity to the often too-serious world of organizational science. With a PhD from the University of California at Berkeley, Dr. Huber doesn't just juggle complex concepts of strategic planning and change management; he makes them dance.

Over the course of 45 consulting projects – yes, he counted – Dr. Huber has reshaped healthcare with a twinkle in his eye, guiding hospital mergers and tech trends with the finesse of a seasoned conductor... if that conductor had a penchant for groundbreaking healthcare initiatives and a good laugh.

Dr. Huber's approach to innovation is akin to mixing a masterful cocktail: one part technology, one part telemedicine, and a generous splash of forward-thinking. His collaborations on future healthcare technologies aren't just about predicting trends; they're about crafting a future where even the robots have a sense of humor.

A scholar with a side of wry wit, Dr. Huber's publications cover the gamut from leadership coaching to the dynamics of healthcare management. His writing isn't just transformative; it's infused with insights that are as thought-provoking as they are chuckle-inducing.

As a researcher and consultant, he's not just fluent in English and German; he's fluent in the language of impactful studies. His work doesn't just earn grants and accolades; it earns nodding heads and the occasional "aha!" moment.

The brainchild of Dr. Huber, Elevate Leadership Coaching, isn't your run-of-the-mill leadership program. It's a blend of organizational science, practical experience, and a secret ingredient – a sense of fun. It's about stretching limits, inspiring change, and the art of leading with both gravitas and a grin.

In a nutshell, Dr. Thomas P. Huber is the Dumbledore of healthcare leadership – wise, slightly whimsical, and with a talent for turning the mundane into the magical. His influence stretches far and wide, proving that leadership, at its best, is not just about growth and excellence, but also about finding joy in the journey.

Elevate Leadership Coaching:

Elevate Leadership Coaching is Dr. Huber's magnum opus, where traditional leadership meets unconventional flair. It's a program that takes academic knowledge, adds a pinch of real-world savvy, and serves it up in a way that's both enlightening and entertaining. Here, leaders learn to not just climb the ladder of success, but to also enjoy the view and maybe even take a selfie or two along the way. At its heart, it's about unlocking potential, nurturing growth, and occasionally, laughing in the face of leadership challenges.

Connect with Dr. Huber at thomaspatrick@mac.com or at https://www.linkedin.com/in/thomaspatrickconsulting/ To learn more about his transformative work with organizations at https://elevateus.ch.

Printed in Great Britain
by Amazon

34124600R00076